# 50 Walks in
# WILTSHIRE

## 50 Walks of 2–10 Miles

# Contents

## The Walks

# Following the Walks

An information panel for each walk shows its relative difficulty, the distance and total amount of ascent. An indication of the gradients you will encounter is shown by the rating ▲▲▲ (no steep slopes) to ▲▲▲ (several very steep slopes). Each walk is rated for its relative difficulty compared to the other walks in this book. Walks marked ✦✦✦ and colour-coded green are likely to be shorter and easier with little total ascent. Those marked with ✦✦✦ and colour-coded orange are of intermediate difficulty. The hardest walks are marked ✦✦✦ and colour-coded red.

## MAPS

There are 40 maps, covering the 50 walks. Some walks have a suggested option in the same area. The information panel for these walks will tell you how much extra walking is involved. On short-cut suggestions the panel will tell you the total distance if you set out from the start of the main walk. Where an option returns to the same point on the main walk, just the distance of the loop is given. Where an option leaves the main walk at one point and returns to it at another, then the distance shown is for the whole walk. The minimum time suggested is for reasonably fit walkers and doesn't allow for stops. Each walk has a suggested map.

## ROUTE MAP LEGEND

| | | | |
|---|---|---|---|
| ⇢ | Walk Route | ▭ | Built-up Area |
| ❶ | Route Waypoint | ▭ | Woodland Area |
| – – – – | Adjoining Path | 👫 | Toilet |
| ⚡ | Viewpoint | 🅿 | Car Park |
| • | Place of Interest | 🪑 | Picnic Area |
| ⌂ | Steep Section | )( | Bridge |

## START POINTS

The start of each walk is given as a six-figure grid reference prefixed by two letters indicating which 100km square of the National Grid it refers to. You'll find more information on grid references on most Ordnance Survey, AA Walking and Leisure Maps.

## DOGS

We have tried to give dog owners useful advice about how dog friendly each walk is. Please respect other countryside users. Keep your dog under control, especially around livestock, and obey local bylaws and other dog control notices.

## CAR PARKING

Many of the car parks suggested are public, but occasionally you may find you have to park on the roadside or in a lay-by. Please be considerate when you leave your car, ensuring that access roads or gates are not blocked and that other vehicles can pass safely.

## WALKS LOCATOR

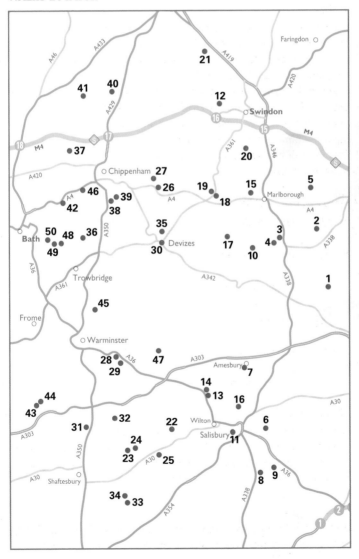

# Walking in Wiltshire

A land shrouded in mystery, myth and legend, Wiltshire evokes images of ancient stone circles, white chalk horses carved into hillsides, crop circles and the forbidden, empty landscape of Salisbury Plain. To many M4 and A303 travellers heading out of London through the clutter of the Thames Valley, Wiltshire is where the landscape opens out and rural England begins.

## WILTSHIRE LANDSCAPES

Wiltshire's charm lies in the beauty of its countryside. The expansive chalk landscapes of the Marlborough and Pewsey downs and Cranborne Chase inspire a sense of space and freedom, offering miles of uninterrupted views deep into Dorset, Somerset and the Cotswolds. South Wiltshire offers the crystal waters of the Ebble, Avon, Nadder and Wylye rivers meandering through tranquil valleys etched into the chalk, linking picture-postcard villages, on their way to Salisbury and its majestic cathedral. Jurassic limestone forms the county's northwest border. This is the southeast edge of the Cotswolds, characterised by its gently undulating landscape and the distinctive, honey-coloured stone buildings.

## ANCIENT ROUTES

Although famous the world over for the prehistoric sites of Avebury and Stonehenge, Wiltshire has much more to offer the walker who is keen to explore the 2,500 miles (4,022km) of public footpaths that criss-cross the county. Several long distance trails pass through Wiltshire, including the Ridgeway, the Thames Path and the Macmillan Way. The circular White Horse Trail visits all Wiltshire's famous white chalk horses in its 90 miles (145km), and the circular, 30-mile (48km) Imber Range Perimeter Path circumnavigates the army's training area on Salisbury Plain.

Many of the routes described in this book traverse sweeping chalk downlands in search of ancient paths, barrows, monoliths and hill-forts, and the best views. You can stride across the sarsen-strewn landscape of Fyfield Down near Marlborough, walk in the footsteps of Civil War soldiers on Roundway Down above Devizes, and locate two of Wiltshire's famous White Horses on Milk Hill and Westbury Hill. Some walks combine invigorating hilltops with tranquil valleys and riverside strolls or tow path walking beside the Kennet and Avon Canal.

## SETTLEMENTS

Wiltshire's thriving market towns and picturesque villages provide interesting starting points and welcome diversions along the way. Stroll through quaint timbered and thatched villages in the southern

*Right: Remains of the settlement at Old Sarum (Walk 16)*

villages of Lacock, Castle Combe and Sherston. Walk around Salisbury and discover architectural styles from the 13th century to the present and take time to visit the city's elegant cathedral and fascinating museums. At Devizes, trace the medieval street pattern and admire some grand buildings before following the Kennet and Avon Canal tow path to the famous Caen Hill flight of 29 locks.

## VISITOR ATTRACTIONS

Wiltshire is richly endowed with manor houses, mansions and beautiful gardens. On these walks, you can stroll past Bowood House, Lacock Abbey and Corsham Court, and enjoy a walk between The Courts at Holt and Great Chalfield Manor. Among the impressive gardens, Stourhead stands out as one of England's finest 18th-century landscaped gardens.

This guide should help you to discover that Wiltshire offers some of the best walking anywhere in lowland, rural England.

PUBLIC TRANSPORT  Wiltshire's good network of bus and rail services provides a convenient way of accessing the county's market towns, villages and tourist attractions. Walks 2, 11, 46, 48/49 and 50 start close to railway stations. For train times call the 24-hour national train information line on 08457 48 49 50. For details of the wide range of public transport services across the county, call the Wiltshire Traveline on 0871 200 22 33. You can also get travel information on the internet at www.transportdirect.info.

*Above: Old Wardour Castle (Walk 23)*

# Walking in Safety

All these walks are suitable for any reasonably fit person, but less experienced walkers should try the easier walks first. Route finding is usually straightforward, but you will find that an Ordnance Survey or AA walking map is a useful addition to the route maps and descriptions; recommendations can be found in the information panels.

## RISKS

Although each walk here has been researched with a view to minimising the risks to the walkers who follow its route, no walk in the countryside can be considered to be completely free from risk. Walking in the outdoors will always require a degree of common sense and judgement to ensure that it is as safe as possible.

- Be particularly careful on cliff paths and in upland terrain, where the consequences of a slip can be very serious.
- Remember to check tidal conditions before walking on the seashore.
- Some sections of route are by, or cross, busy roads. Take care and remember traffic is a danger even on minor country lanes.
- Be careful around farmyard machinery and livestock, especially if you have children with you.
- Be aware of the consequences of changes in the weather and check the forecast before you set out. Carry spare clothing and a torch if you are walking in the winter months. Remember the weather can change very quickly at any time of the year, and in moorland and heathland areas, mist and fog can make route finding much harder. Don't set out in these conditions unless you are confident of your navigation skills in poor visibility. In summer remember to take account of the heat and sun; wear a hat and carry water.
- On walks away from centres of population you should carry a whistle and survival bag. If you do have an accident requiring the emergency services, make a note of your position as accurately as possible and dial 999.

## COUNTRYSIDE CODE

- Be safe, plan ahead and follow any signs.
- Leave gates and property as you find them.
- Protect plants and animals and take your litter home.
- Keep dogs under close control.
- Consider other people.

For more information visit www.naturalengland.org.uk/ourwork/enjoying/countrysidecode

*Overleaf: The Kennet and Avon Canal at Great Bedwyn (Walk 2)*

# Around the Chutes

DISTANCE 8 miles (12.9km)   MINIMUM TIME 4hrs

ASCENT/GRADIENT 1,099ft (335m) ▲▲▲   LEVEL OF DIFFICULTY +++

PATHS Bridle paths, downland tracks, field paths, roads

LANDSCAPE Farmland, woodland, downland pasture, village streets

SUGGESTED MAP OS Explorer 131 Romsey, Andover & Test Valley

START/FINISH Grid reference: SU308530

DOG FRIENDLINESS Lead required around farmland and on road

PARKING Lower Chute Club

PUBLIC TOILETS None on route

This walk explores the hilly and relatively deserted border country between Wiltshire and Hampshire in what remains of Chute Forest. In medieval times vast tracts of woodland canopied an area from Savernake Forest in the north to Salisbury in the south, before swelling out into the New Forest, providing a prime hunting ground.

## THE CHUTES

The parishes of Chute and Chute Forest can be traced back to Norman times. Deforestation began in 1632 under Charles I (1600–49), who divided the area up among his favoured nobles. The result of this is still evident today in the form of five small hamlets – Upper and Lower Chute, Chute Standen, Chute Forest and Chute Cadley – which developed around what were once farms or country houses.

The landscape is still well wooded with a mixture of copse, plantations, windbreaks or 'rows' and roadside plantings of beech linked by hedgerow trees. The paths and byways on this walk explore this quite remote area of Wiltshire, which rises to over 800ft (244m), giving splendid views south across Hampshire to the Isle of Wight. The highest point is on the impressive Chute Causeway, originally part of the Roman highway from Winchester in Hampshire to Mildenhall, near Marlborough. It forms a great arc around some of the most attractive scenery in Wiltshire, for just north of the now-paved road are deep combes (such as Hippenscombe Bottom) and steep hills (such as Knolls Down). Even the Roman road, which usually ignores natural obstacles, swerves to avoid them. At the eastern end of the Causeway is early 19th-century Conholt House. It was here, during excavations in 1898, that a small terrace set with 12–16 inches (30–41cm) of flint was uncovered. Part of this terrace appears to have been burned, which offers an explanation as to how the Romans built such straight roads – by lighting fires at both ends of the semicircular section of the Causeway they could line up the columns of smoke to align their road.

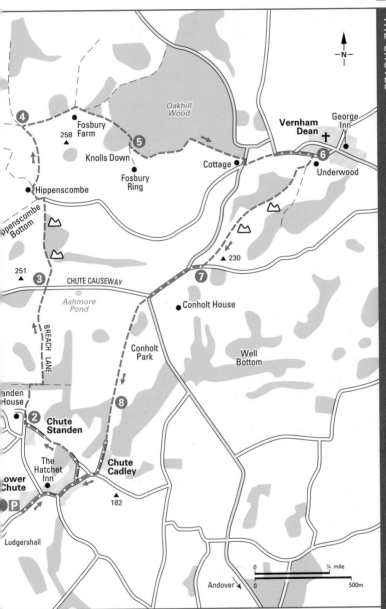

**1** Turn left out of the car park and then right at the T-junction. Fork left at the war memorial, then turn left again by the 'Chute Cadley' village sign. Keep left and take the bridle path, a track, through the edge of woodland. Continue between hedgerows and descend into Chute Standen.

**2** Turn right at the T-junction, then, where the lane swings left to Standen House, keep straight on up a grassy track of Breach Lane. At the T-junction, turn right and then left along the edge of woodland. Continue for 0.5 miles (800m) to Chute Causeway.

**3** Cross straight over the causeway and later steeply descend the track to a metalled lane in Hippenscombe Bottom. Turn left, then right and swing right, then left between farm buildings. Fork right along a grassy track (passing to the right of a long, breeze-block barn), which soon swings left, and steadily ascend to a crossing of ways.

**4** Turn sharp right along the gravel track. At Fosbury Farm, bear right and walk beside woodland. Follow the track into the woods and, as you leave the woods, cross a stile by a gate and briefly leave the marked route to pass through the ancient earthworks into Fosbury Ring on top of Knolls Down.

**5** Fork left on a grassy track never far from the woodland. Pass to the right of a tiny screened pond, then swing left on a track, exit the ring and walk down the left-hand field-edge. Cross the stile in the corner and go around the left edge of a large field. Descend to a cottage in the corner. Turn right along the lane and go through the kissing gate almost immediately on your left. Keep to the right-hand field-edge to a kissing gate and road and turn right into Vernham Dean.

**6** Take the waymarked fenced track beside a house called Underwood. The fencing on the right ends just before a gap; here turn right along a hedged track. Follow the track just within woodland, then follow the waymarkers carefully, steeply uphill across a field and through a small plantation to a gap. Turn left along the top of the escarpment to a gate in the corner on to the road.

**7** Turn right, then, where the road swings sharp left by a junction, keep straight on through a gate. Initially head towards an open-sided barn, but then bear left across a depression and continue to another stile. Cross the next field to a stile and walk down a track between fields. Bear slightly left, then walk along the right-hand field-edge to enter a long, narrow field, bounded by woodland.

**8** Keep to the right-hand edge and go by a redundant stile on the right just before the corner. Continue beside woodland, soon joining a drive which becomes a metalled lane. Turn right at the T-junction and go forward (not forking right) to retrace your steps back to the car park.

**WHERE TO EAT AND DRINK** Time your walk to coincide with opening time at The Hatchet inn in Lower Chute, a thatched 16th-century pub with low beams, a log fire and home-cooked food. Along the way, try the George Inn in Vernham Dean for Greene King ales and traditional pub food.

**WHAT TO SEE** Explore Knolls Down and the ramparts of Fosbury Ring, an oval bivallate hill-fort from the Iron Age with views west along Hippenscombe Bottom into the heart of Wiltshire.

**WHILE YOU'RE THERE** Visit the ruins of Ludgershall Castle, built during the late 11th century and later used by Henry III. It fell into decay around the 16th century, but you can still see some of the original large Norman earthworks.

# Great Bedwyn and the Kennet and Avon Canal

| | |
|---|---|
| DISTANCE 6.75 miles (10.9km) | MINIMUM TIME 2hrs |

ASCENT/GRADIENT 147ft (45m) ▲▲▲    LEVEL OF DIFFICULTY ✦✦✦

PATHS Field paths, woodland tracks, tow path, roads

LANDSCAPE Farmland, woodland, canal and village scenery

SUGGESTED MAP OS Explorer 157 Marlborough & Savernake Forest

START/FINISH Grid reference: SU279645

DOG FRIENDLINESS Lead required on wooded sections and road

PARKING Great Bedwyn Station

PUBLIC TOILETS Crofton Pumping Station

Situated beside a peaceful stretch of the Kennet and Avon Canal, the large village of Great Bedwyn was formerly a market town. It still has the appearance of a small town with a wide main street, a few elegant town houses and the flint Church of St Mary the Virgin.

## KENNET AND AVON CANAL

The main reason to visit Great Bedwyn is to enjoy the Kennet and Avon Canal and the beautiful scenery it meanders through. It was in 1788 that the idea of linking the River Kennet with the River Avon at Bath by means of an artificial waterway was first mooted. The navigation between the rivers had to rise to 450ft (137m), then descend on the other side, and needed 104 locks, two aqueducts and, at the summit, a tunnel over 500yds (457m) long. Construction started in 1794 and was completed in 1810. The canal was used to carry coal from the Somerset coalfield, iron, stone and slate, local agricultural products and timber, and to bring luxuries like tobacco and spirits from London to Bath, Bristol and the intervening towns.

Transporting goods along the canal was successful for 40 years, but with railways offering more efficient transport, it fell into decline. The Kennet and Avon Canal Trust and British Waterways have revitalised the navigable waterway, making the banks and tow paths accessible to anglers, naturalists and walkers. A highlight of the walk along the tow path are the magnificent beam engines at Crofton Pumping Station.

## WILTON WINDMILL

The county's only complete surviving working windmill stands on a hilltop overlooking the canal. Built in 1821, it is a five-storey brick tower mill and was fully operational until the 1890s. It closed and became derelict in the 1920s, but was restored in the 1970s.

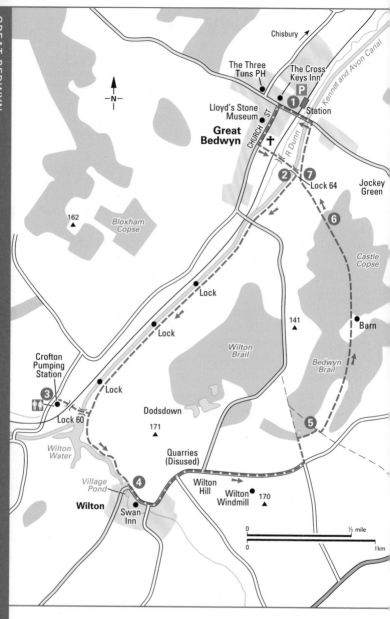

**Great Bedwyn**

① Walk to the main road in Great Bedwyn. Turn right, then left down Church Street. Pass the post office and church, then take the footpath left between two graveyards. Climb a stile, cross a field to a kissing gate, then carefully cross the railway line to another kissing gate. Cross the footbridge, then the bridge over the canal and descend to the tow path.

② Turn right, pass beneath the bridge and continue along the tow path for 1.5 miles (2.4km), passing three locks and through two gates, to reach Lock 60. Go through a gate and cross the canal here, turn left, then follow a path right and pass through the tunnel beneath the railway. Ascend steps to the Crofton Pumping Station.

**3** Retrace your steps back to the tow path and Lock 60. Turn left for a few paces, then take the footpath right, waymarked to Wilton Windmill, and walk beside Wilton Water along the edge of fields. Eventually, turn right down a short track to a lane by the village pond in Wilton.

**4** Turn left, then just past the Swan Inn, follow the lane left and uphill through trees. Climb out of the village and turn right to pass close to Wilton Windmill. Continue along the lane and turn left on to a track, opposite the lane to Hungerford. Just before the wooded track snakes downhill, turn right above a pond along a bridle path (unsigned) beside woodland.

**5** At a staggered crossing of paths, turn right, then in 50yds (46m), turn

left. Go down a well-surfaced track and through a gate into Bedwyn Brail. Continue though the woods, following signs to Great Bedwyn. The hard track gives way to a grassy track – follow this along a clearing and bear left across a clearing before forking left at a barn to re-enter the woods in the left-hand corner of the clearing.

**6** On emerging in a field corner, keep left along the field boundary. Go through a gap in the hedge and descend along the left-hand side of the next field, with Great Bedwyn visible ahead. Near the bottom of the field, bear half right, downhill to the canal.

**7** Pass through a gate by a bridge and Lock 64 and turn right along the tow path. Go through the car park to the road, then turn left over the canal and rail bridges before turning right back to Great Bedwyn Station.

**WHERE TO EAT AND DRINK** Great Bedwyn has two pubs, The Cross Keys Inn and The Three Tuns, and a bakery. Light refreshments are available if visiting the Crofton Beam Engines, while at Wilton the homely Swan Inn offers meals made with locally sourced produce, snacks, good Sunday lunches and a selection of real ales.

**WHAT TO SEE** In St Mary's Church, Great Bedwyn, look for the tomb of Sir John Seymour in the chancel. His daughter Jane was Henry VIII's third and best-loved wife.

**WHILE YOU'RE THERE** The post office buildings in Great Bedwyn are adorned with monuments, gravestones and sculpture dating back to the 18th century, all fine examples of the stonemason's art. Just north of Great Bedwyn is Chisbury Camp, an ancient hill-fort with the ruins of a 13th-century chapel standing within its 50ft (15m) high earth ramparts.

*Overleaf: Thatched cottages in Great Bedwyn (Walk 2)*

# Savernake's Royal Forest

| | |
|---|---|
| **DISTANCE** 9 miles (14.5km) | **MINIMUM TIME** 4hrs |

**ASCENT/GRADIENT** 213ft (65m) ▲▲▲    **LEVEL OF DIFFICULTY** ✚✚✚

**PATHS** Woodland tracks, tow path, bridle paths, country lanes

**LANDSCAPE** Forest, farmland, canal

**SUGGESTED MAP** OS Explorer 157 Marlborough & Savernake Forest

**START/FINISH** Grid reference: SU215646

**DOG FRIENDLINESS** Parts of Savernake Forest have signs requesting dogs be kept on lead; off lead along tow path

**PARKING** Hat Gate 8 picnic area off A346 south of Marlborough

**PUBLIC TOILETS** None on route

**NOTES** There are thieves in the area – be sure not to leave valuables on display

On a chalk plateau above Marlborough on the northeast edge of Salisbury Plain, Savernake consists of 2,750 acres (1,114ha) of mixed woodland managed by the Forestry Commission. In the Middle Ages it was a wilderness of bracken and heathland and had been a royal hunting ground long before the Norman Conquest. It was William the Conqueror who appointed the first hereditary warden, Richard Esturmy, and subsequent kings of England hunted deer in the forest glades.

## THE SEYMOURS

In the 15th century a daughter of the Esturmy family married into the Seymour family who became wardens of Savernake. In 1535, Jane Seymour was introduced to King Henry VIII by her father, Sir John. Jane's brother, Edward, became warden in 1536 and was created Protector of the Realm, the Duke of Somerset, on Henry VIII's death in 1547. He persuaded Henry's successor King Edward to transfer the ownership of Savernake to the Seymour family. In 1676 it passed by marriage to the Bruce family and so to the present owner, the Marquis of Ailesbury. Tottenham House was first built in 1742, but the existing (and fourth) construction was built in 1820.

## EIGHTEENTH-CENTURY LANDSCAPING

Although a large part of the forest was enclosed during the early 17th century, much of it decayed due to the lack of replanting following timber demands for shipbuilding. Today's forest was the inspiration of 'Capability' Brown. He planned the 4-mile (6.4km) Grand Avenue that cuts north to south, and the eight lesser beech avenues leading to the forest centre. Originally intended to be formal, it now has an air of informality, with young broad-leaved trees and tall pines intermingling with the surviving great beeches and ancient pollarded oaks.

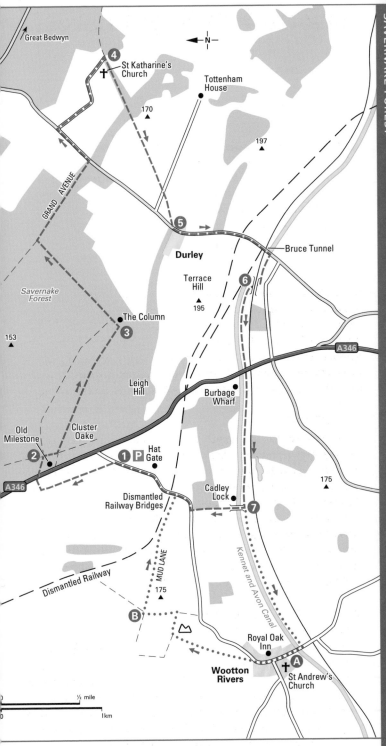

Great Bedwyn

4 St Katharine's
Church

N

Tottenham
House

170

197

GRAND AVENUE

5

**Durley**

Bruce Tunnel

Savernake
Forest

Terrace
Hill

195

6

The Column

3

153

Leigh
Hill

A346

Burbage
Wharf

Old
Milestone

Cluster
Oake

175

2

1 P Hat
Gate

Cadley
Lock

7

A346

Dismantled
Railway Bridges

MUD LANE

Dismantled Railway

175

Kennet and Avon Canal

B

Royal Oak
Inn

½ mile

**Wootton
Rivers**

A

St Andrew's
Church

1km

**1** From the car park, turn right, then almost immediately left past a wooden barrier. Follow the wooded path for 500yds (457m), then bear right to reach the A346. Cross over near an old milestone and take the track beyond a wooden barrier, signed to Tottenham House.

**2** In 150yds (137m), at a major crossing of routes, turn right and, after a similar distance, keep left at a junction where the path runs straight on. Follow this straight track (which can be very muddy in places) for 0.75 miles (1.2km) to The Column.

**3** Approaching it, turn left and follow the track for 0.8 miles (1.25km) to a junction with Grand Avenue. Turn right and follow it for 0.5 miles (800m) to the road. Turn left, pass Warren Lodge and take the next right turning for St Katharine's Church.

**4** Beyond the church turn right at the sign for Durley. Pass through trees and beyond a gate, then continue to a stile beyond the woodland. Walk ahead and over another stile. Cross parkland and woodland and the drive to Tottenham House, then cross a stile to open parkland and go over another stile and continue to the road.

**5** Turn left, walk through the hamlet of Durley and keep to the lane across the old railway bridge, then the main railway bridge, and shortly take the footpath on the right, waymarked 'Wootton Rivers'. You are now walking above the Kennet and Avon Canal as it passes through the Bruce Tunnel.

**6** Walk down some steps, pass through a narrow and low tunnel under the railway line and join the canal tow path just below the entrance to the Bruce Tunnel. Turn left along the tow path for about 1.5 miles (2.4km), passing beneath the A346 at Burbage Wharf to reach Cadley Lock.

**7** Turn right over bridge No. 105 and follow the metalled track to a T-junction. Turn right and keep to the road, passing two dismantled railway bridges, back to the car park at Hat Gate.

WHERE TO EAT AND DRINK The 16th-century, thatched and timber-framed Royal Oak Inn at Wootton Rivers offers a good range of interesting pub food and real ales. It's worth undertaking the extra few miles as this walk is devoid of a refreshment stop.

WHAT TO SEE You may catch a glimpse of fallow deer as you walk through Savernake Forest. Well-lit clearings may be carpeted with snowdrops or primroses and the woods with bluebells, while wood anemones, wood sorrel and rosebay willowherb thrive in spring and early summer.

WHILE YOU'RE THERE Drive east towards Great Bedwyn to see the steam-powered beam engines at Crofton Pumping Station, or visit Wiltshire's only operating windmill at Wilton (see Walk 2). Visit St Katharine's Church, near Durley, a chapel of ease to the mother church of Great Bedwyn and dedicated by the Marchioness of Ailesbury in memory of her Russian mother, the Dowager Countess of Pembroke.

# Wootton Rivers

DISTANCE 11.75 miles (18.9km)    MINIMUM TIME 4hrs 30min

ASCENT/GRADIENT 279ft (85m) ▲▲▲    LEVEL OF DIFFICULTY ✦✦✦

SEE MAP AND INFORMATION PANEL FOR WALK 3

At Point ❼, don't cross the bridge, instead keep to the canal tow path and pass three further locks to reach bridge No. 108 at Wootton Rivers. Leave the tow path and turn right across the bridge into the village.

The section of the Kennet and Avon Canal from Wootton Rivers to the western portal of the Bruce Tunnel includes the Wootton Rivers flight of four locks, which raise the canal 35ft (11m) to its summit level of 450ft (137m) compared to 65ft (20m) in Bath. Beyond the 502yd (459m) long Bruce Tunnel and Crofton Pumping Station, the canal descends gradually all the way to the Thames at Reading.

Wootton Rivers is a classic Wiltshire village. Essentially a linear settlement, it is particularly pretty with its mile-long (1.6km) main street composed almost entirely of timber-framed, thatched cottages and brick houses.

As you stroll gently uphill away from the canal and its restored lock and keeper's cottage, take the long enclosed pathway on your left to visit St Andrew's Church, which stands close to the impressive manor house. Of particular interest is the clock

in the wooden belfry. Built in 1911 to commemorate the Coronation of George V, it is unique in having three faces. Two are conventional, the third (south facing) displays the words 'Glory be to God' around the edge of the dial instead of numerals. It was designed by the amusingly named Jack Spratt, an eccentric countryman and amateur clockmaker, out of donations of mechanical junk, old prams, bicycles and bedsteads as the people of the village could not afford to buy one. It is said to have a repertoire of 24 chimes.

Pass St Andrew's Church, Point ❹, on your left, and the Royal Oak Inn on your right, then, as the road swings right, take the waymarked bridle path left by the house called Martinsell. Follow this tree-lined track, which climbs to a T-junction of routes at the top of the hill. Turn right, then, in the field corner, turn left and in 50yds (46m) go through the field hedge to join the track on your right. Turn left and ascend to a further T-junction, Point ❺. Turn right down Mud Lane, a wooded track, eventually reaching a metalled lane in 0.5 miles (800m). Turn left along the lane back to Hat Gate car park.

# Ramsbury

| | |
|---|---|
| DISTANCE | 6.5 miles (10.4km)    MINIMUM TIME 2hrs |
| ASCENT/GRADIENT | 229ft (70m) ▲▲▲    LEVEL OF DIFFICULTY ✛✛✛ |
| PATHS | Field paths and established tracks |
| LANDSCAPE | Farmland, woodland, parkland, village streets |
| SUGGESTED MAP | OS Explorers 157 Marlborough & Savernake; 158 Newbury & Hungerford |
| START/FINISH | Grid reference: SU274715 (on Explorer 157) |
| DOG FRIENDLINESS | Keep dogs under control at all times |
| PARKING | Roadside parking near church in Ramsbury |
| PUBLIC TOILETS | In front of church in Ramsbury |

Ramsbury nestles on a wide stretch of the River Kennet close to the Berkshire border. Between AD 908 and 1058 it was the centre of a flourishing diocese, complete with cathedral and bishop, before it was transferred to preferred Sherborne and later to Old Sarum. Although a mere parish for more than nine centuries, the village has an impressive church built on Anglo-Saxon foundations.

## MYSTERIES OF LITTLECOTE HOUSE

With parts dating back to the 13th century, Littlecote is an exquisite manor house standing amid spacious lawns and gardens, with the River Kennet running through the surrounding parkland. Behind the building's long, gabled Elizabethan facade are some fine architectural treasures, notably the 110ft (33.5m) Long Gallery, the oak-panelled Great Hall and the magnificent Cromwellian chapel, probably the only complete example of its kind in England.

Among the regular sightings of ghosts have been that of a mother and her baby, a midwife and 'Wild' Will Darrell, who owned the estate in the mid-16th century. It is said that he had many mistresses, including his own sister whom he made pregnant. One night he called for a midwife to assist at the birth She delivered the child and gave it to Darrell who immediately threw it on the fire. Her conscience troubled her and she told the local magistrate. Darrell was brought to trial, accused of murder, before Judge Popham, but was acquitted after bribing Popham with the offer of Littlecote House.

## THE ORPHEUS MOSAIC

William George, steward of Littlecote Park, unearthed the remains of the Roman villa which lies to the west of the mansion, in the early 18th century. Edward Popham, the owner, allowed George to make detailed drawings of the mosaic floor before ordering it to be buried again to avoid publicity. George died shortly afterwards and it was thought that the mosaic had been destroyed until it was rediscovered by archaeologists in 1978. Excavations have continued over the 3-acre (1.2ha) site, but you will find the showpiece of the villa, the superb Orpheus mosaic, beautifully restored and relaid in its original position (under a sheltering roof). Dating from around AD 360, it plays an important role in our understanding of early Christian architecture.

**1** From the church, walk east to the Square and The Bell pub. Bear right down Scholards Lane, signed to Hungerford. At the road junction turn right, signed 'Froxfield', and cross the Kennet. Continue ahead up the road.

**2** Just before a cottage, take the metalled track left, waymarked to Littlecote House. As the drive bears right, continue straight on along a track through the valley. In 0.5 miles (800m) pass a cottage called West Lodge, and continue ahead on the grassy path. Keep left along the field-edge, parallel with the river.

**3** As the end of Littlecote House comes into view, hook back left down the metalled track to explore the foundations of the Roman villa and the remarkably preserved mosaic. Return to the junction of paths and turn left, walking past the front of the magnificent old mansion and straight on down the drive, with its avenue of trees, to reach a gatehouse and road.

**4** Turn right, ascend the steep lane, then, where it turns sharp left, keep straight on through the hotel entrance gates, signed 'Ramsbury'. As the metalled track swings right, go straight ahead along the gravelled track. Pass a collection of fancy chickens and go straight ahead through a field gate, following the track ahead.

**5** At a junction of tracks, fork right along a concrete track, following the bridle path uphill. Keep right, and where the concrete track swings right into woodland near the top of the hill, take the path ahead just within the woodland fringe. The path soon veers right, descends into the valley and follows the left-hand edge of a field to reach the track by the cottage encountered on the outward route. Turn left to reach the road (Point **2**). Cross straight over and walk ahead along the bridleway track.

**6** Pass between two cottages and turn sharp right. Follow the footpath over two bridges, passing the weir. Keep ahead on the lane into Ramsbury, then turn right along the high street to return to the start point by the church.

WHERE TO EAT AND DRINK  The Bell, which overlooks the Square, is a smartly refurbished former coaching inn, offering fine accommodation and dining. It provides a stylish and innovative menu and simpler, yet equally appetising lunchtime bar meals and offers good changing ales, decent wines and a sheltered rear garden.

WHAT TO SEE  Ramsbury Manor, a handsome brick building of nine bays, built in 1680 by John Webb, son-in-law of Inigo Jones, takes advantage of its fine riverside setting. It was here that Oliver Cromwell (1599–1658) laid his plans for the subjugation of Ireland.

WHILE YOU'RE THERE  Follow the walk with a leisurely drive to the attractive market town of Marlborough. A borough since 1204, it has a very wide main street lined with some fine 18th-century houses. The Polly Tea Rooms with its afternoon teas provides perfect post-walk refreshment.

# Clarendon's Lost Palace

DISTANCE 7.5 miles (12.1km)    MINIMUM TIME 3hrs

ASCENT/GRADIENT 410ft (125m) ▲▲▲    LEVEL OF DIFFICULTY +++

PATHS Field paths, woodland tracks, country lanes, many stiles

LANDSCAPE Gently undulating farmland and woodland

SUGGESTED MAP OS Explorers 131 Romsey, Andover & Test Valley and 130 Salisbury & Stonehenge

START/FINISH Grid reference: SU212312 (on Explorer 131)

DOG FRIENDLINESS Keep dogs under control across farmland

PARKING Considerate roadside parking in Pitton

PUBLIC TOILETS None on route

The parish of Pitton and Farley lies on the boundary of Clarendon Park, which occupies a wide arc of country due east of Salisbury. In Saxon times the area was covered with an ancient forest and within its bounds are the remains of the once magnificent Clarendon Palace, which began its life as a Saxon hunting lodge. It was expanded by the Plantagenets into a great country house becoming, in the 14th century, second only to the Palace of Westminster in size and importance.

## ROYAL RESIDENCE

Henry II and Henry III were both responsible for creating this grand building. Many great names in history visited the palace, notably Thomas Beckett and the captive kings, John of France and David of Scotland. It continued to be a residence of the royal family until the outbreak of the War of the Roses in 1455. At the end of the conflict in 1485, although in decline, the palace was sustained and occasionally visited by Yorkist, Tudor and Stuart monarchs until the land and the now almost ruined building were confiscated by Parliament following the execution of Charles I in 1649.

Archaeologist Dr Tancred Borenius excavated the site in the 1930s, revealing evidence of a Saxon building below Norman foundations. You can now view the results of the ongoing excavations that are beginning to reveal the hidden history and glory of this once magnificent palace.

Just south of Pitton is Farley, a fragmented settlement built around a triangle of lanes with a pleasant assortment of buildings. It is known for its classical church, built of country brick in a style influenced by Sir Christopher Wren. It was built for Sir Stephen Fox who was born in Farley of poor parentage, but being an able and intelligent man he served Charles II, eventually rising to the post of Paymaster General. Fox later bought Farley Manor and employed Alexander Fort to build the village church between 1689 and 1690.

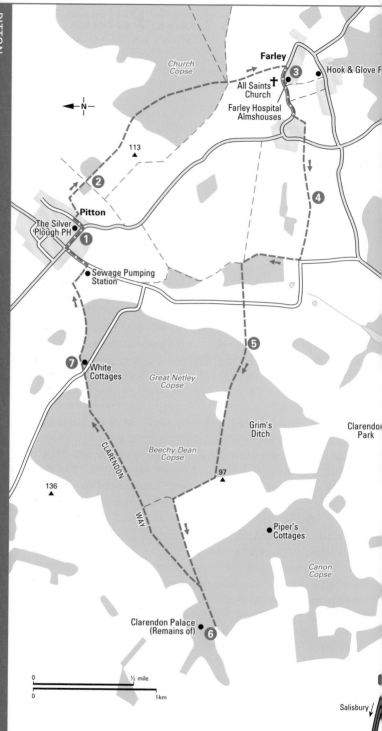

Church
Copse

**Farley**

Hook & Glove F

**3**

All Saints
Church

Farley Hospital
Almshouses

←—N—

113

**4**

**2**

**Pitton**

The Silver
Plough PH

**1**

Sewage Pumping
Station

**5**

**7** White
Cottages

*Great Netley
Copse*

Grim's
Ditch

Clarendo
Park

CLARENDON

*Beechy Dean
Copse*

97

136

WAY

Piper's
Cottages

*Canon
Copse*

Clarendon Palace
(Remains of)

**6**

0                    ½ mile

0                              1km

Salisbury

**1** Locate The Silver Plough pub and walk up a cul-de sac to the right of it. In 100yds (91m), take the footpath right, heading uphill between houses to a stile. Go across a narrow field to a stile, then go ahead along the right-hand field-edge to a stile by a gate.

**2** Cross the track and continue ahead along another track to the right of woodland. It narrows and soon reaches a narrow gap. Keep ahead, cross a stile and enter Church Copse. Stay ahead on the main track to the right. Follow this straight on and down, with a fence to your right. Where the fenced path joins a track bear right, then, at a junction on the woodland fringe, keep straight on downhill into Farley village.

**3** At the road, turn right and pass All Saints Church and the almshouses. Leave the village and take the third path on the left, over a stile (the second is opposite the Coronation playing fields). Go diagonally right and follow the hedge right to a stile by a bungalow. Walk down the drive, cross the lane to a gate and follow the path through a long field to a stile and gate.

**4** Proceed across the next field (on the left of power cables) to a stile and gate. Take the track immediately right and follow this byway to a track T-junction with a footpath into a field on the right. Turn left alongside a fenced enclosure and, on emerging from the wood, head straight across two fields and enter further woodland.

**5** Walk through the woodland alongside a clearing to your right and cross a lane back into woodland. Leave the wood and follow the track right, then left around the field-edge and soon re-enter the wood. Keep ahead where the Clarendon Way merges from the right and continue to the ruins of Clarendon Palace.

**6** From the palace remains, retrace your steps through the wood, this time keeping left along the Clarendon Way. Follow the path for nearly a mile (1.6km) through the wood. On emerging, keep straight on down the track and cross the lane by a barn.

**7** Pass beside white cottages and woodland to your right, then walk down a fenced path, soon to bear right to the sewage pumping station. Cross at the bridge, and at the lane turn left, then right, back to the village hall.

**WHERE TO EAT AND DRINK** The Silver Plough in Pitton offers an extensive range of home-made food using local produce. In Farley, the path alongside Farley Hospital Almshouses leads across two fields to the Hook & Glove.

**WHAT TO SEE** Note the brick-built, long and low Farley Hospital Almshouses, designed in 1681 by Alexander Fort, an architect who had worked with Wren, for Sir Stephen Fox, 10 years before he built the church.

# Amesbury and the Woodford Valley

| | |
|---|---|
| DISTANCE 6.5 miles (10.4km) | MINIMUM TIME 2hrs 30min |
| ASCENT/GRADIENT 518ft (158m) ▲▲▲ | LEVEL OF DIFFICULTY ✦✦✦ |

PATHS Tracks, field and bridle paths, roads

LANDSCAPE River valley and chalk downland

SUGGESTED MAP OS Explorer 130 Salisbury & Stonehenge

START/FINISH Grid reference: SU149411

DOG FRIENDLINESS Keep dogs on lead through villages and water-meadows

PARKING Amesbury Recreation Ground car park (free) at end of Recreation Road, off route to West Amesbury

PUBLIC TOILETS Amesbury

Amesbury is a pleasant market town set in a bend of the River Avon, which is crossed by a five-arched bridge built in Palladian style. Its proximity to the eastern edge of Salisbury Plain means that the neighbourhood is dominated by large military camps, including the experimental flying base of Boscombe Down. Despite this, the lesser-known chalk downland and the beautiful Woodford Valley to the south of the town remain delightfully unspoilt. It is perfect walking country with archaeological treasures such as Bronze Age barrows and of course Stonehenge, and chocolate-box villages.

## AMESBURY ABBEY

According to legend, Amesbury was founded by an uncle of King Arthur, a Roman Briton named Ambrosius Aurelianus, hence the name Amesbury. After Arthur's death in the 6th century AD, it is said that Guinevere sought refuge in the Wessex region, probably retreating to Amesbury Abbey. The abbey was succeeded in AD 979 by a nunnery, which became the richest in England. It achieved fame as the refuge of Mary, daughter of Edward I, and her grandmother Queen Eleanor, Henry III's widow. After the Dissolution of the Monasteries in 1540, the convent was demolished and a house was built on the site. This was replaced in 1661 by a new mansion, designed by John Webb in the style of Inigo Jones, his father-in-law. Here, the Duchess of Queensberry inspired John Gay to write *The Beggar's Opera* (1728).

The present Amesbury Abbey was rebuilt in 1840 by Thomas Hopper for Sir Edward Antrobus, owner of the Stonehenge Estate, and is now a nursing home. Amesbury's ancient church is all that remains of the original abbey. Built by the Saxons and remodelled by the Normans, it has a fine example of an early 14th-century window in the chancel, striking tracery and carved bosses.

The River Avon meanders south from Amesbury for 7 miles (11.3km), flowing through the Woodford Valley to Salisbury in the Avon Valley. It is the perfect setting for some of Wiltshire's finest villages, notably the three Woodfords and Great Durnford, with its converted mill, picture-postcard thatched cottages with flower-filled gardens, impressive Norman church and handsome manor house. Take time to visit the church and, if the pub is open, relax with a pint in the garden, which overlooks the lush water-meadows.

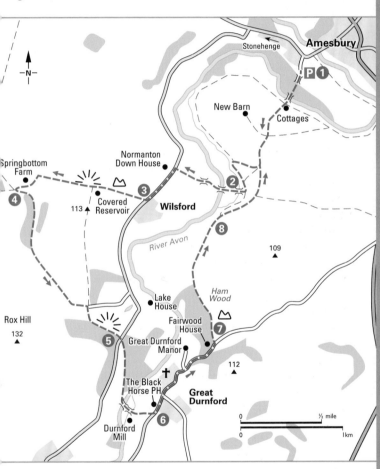

❶ Take the footpath to the right of the play area, cross a footbridge and bear right to cross the main footbridge over the River Avon. At a crossing of tracks, take the track straight ahead, passing to the right of cottages. Head uphill to a junction and go straight on, downhill to a gate. Turn right along the field-edge and bear left in the corner to join a path that passes through the valley bottom beside a stream to shortly cross a footbridge on your right.

❷ Follow the path through marshy ground to cross a bridge over the Avon. Bear right over a small bridge and keep left through a paddock beside the thatched cob wall of a farm to a gate. Bear right along the fenced path beside the drive to the road. Turn left then, in 0.25 miles (400m), reach a right turn.

❸ Either walk up the tarmac road towards Springbottom Farm or join the path through the spinney on your right for views across to Stonehenge. Pass a covered reservoir and some barns, then descend to the farm complex. Just beyond the barns, bear left with a red byway arrow on to a track beside paddocks.

❹ Keep to this track through the downland valley (Lake Bottom) for nearly one mile (1.6km). Where it becomes metalled take the arrowed path right, between new fences, into woodland and bear left uphill. Cross a stile and continue ahead. Once out of the trees, keep right along the field-edge, with views left to Lake House, to a stile.

❺ Cross the lane and take the bridle path right in front of a thatched house. Go past (not through) a gap on your left, to descend gently. Cross a drive and bear left to cross two footbridges over the Avon. Pass beside Durnford Mill and follow the drive out to the lane.

❻ Turn left and walk through Great Durnford, passing the church and drive to Great Durnford Manor, following the public road right, uphill through woodland. Descend and take the waymarked bridle path left beside Fairwood House.

❼ Ascend steeply through the edge of Ham Wood. On leaving the wood, do not curve left and down; bear right along a narrow path through scrub to a gate. Keep right along two fenced field-edges to a gate.

❽ Maintain your direction through the pastureland, not losing height, eventually easing right towards a field boundary corner. Continue for 0.25 miles (400m), following a field-edge. Keeping this line, descend the field-edge to a gate to rejoin your outward route. Retrace your steps back into Amesbury and the car park.

WHERE TO EAT AND DRINK The Black Horse in Great Durnford has a range of ales and a varied bar menu. Amesbury has several cafes and pubs, including The Friar Tuck Café and Antrobus Arms Hotel.

WHAT TO SEE As you climb up the downs away from Wilsford there's a distant view of Stonehenge and the extensive prehistoric landscape of Normanton Down, littered with earthworks and burial mounds. Lake House, a 16th-century mansion, is now home to rock musician Sting.

WHILE YOU'RE THERE Two miles (3.2km) west of Amesbury (off the A303) stands Stonehenge, the most famous prehistoric monument in Europe and a World Heritage Site. Enjoy an audio tour and discover its history and legends. Sadly, in the interests of conservation, you'll have to view it from a distance. Less busy and pre-dating Stonehenge is Woodhenge (off the A345 north of Amesbury), once a ritual temple aligned with sunrise on Midsummer Day.

# Avon Valley from Downton

| | |
|---|---|
| DISTANCE 4.5 miles (7.2km) | MINIMUM TIME 2hrs 30min |

ASCENT/GRADIENT 229ft (70m) ▲▲▲    LEVEL OF DIFFICULTY ✚✚

PATHS Riverside paths, downland tracks, metalled lanes, several stiles

LANDSCAPE River valley, woodland, downland pasture, village streets

SUGGESTED MAP AA Leisure Map 4 New Forest

START/FINISH Grid reference: SU180214

DOG FRIENDLINESS Keep dogs under control across pasture; care needed at A36

PARKING Plenty of roadside parking in High Street

PUBLIC TOILETS None on route

Close to the Hampshire border and straddling the channels of the River Avon south of Salisbury, Downton has the air of a small town about it. Despite this, the central area, known as The Borough, with its wide and pretty green and thatched timber-framed cottages, has not lost its village feel. This is the medieval Downton, built as a 'new town' by the Bishop of Winchester around 1205 close to The Moot, an earthwork that was once the site of a palace built in 1138 by Henry de Blois for the Bishops of Winchester. Gracing this historic plot is Moot House, an 18th-century mansion set in landscaped grounds that include an amphitheatre, lily pond and viewpoint. Near by stands the Manor House, formerly the parsonage, an Elizabethan house once owned by the Raleigh family.

Downton was made a borough in the 13th century, entitling the town to hold markets and fairs. It continued to prosper as industry and commerce flourished. Lace was produced as a cottage industry here, and the village has long been associated with flour- and paper-milling. From 1885 Wiggins Teape Carter and Barlow produced handmade paper until the end of World War I. For centuries the village has supported thriving trout fisheries and today Downton is renowned as an angling centre for the Wiltshire Avon.

## ADMIRAL NELSON'S HOUSE

Over the River Avon, east of Charlton All Saints, is a large mansion in parkland. Dating back to the 18th century, and once known as Standlynch House, it was acquired by the Treasury in 1814 and renamed Trafalgar House after being given to the heirs of Admiral Viscount Nelson. The Nelson family lived here until 1948. In the redundant chapel, now sadly boarded up, the Nelson name appears on some of the gravestones.

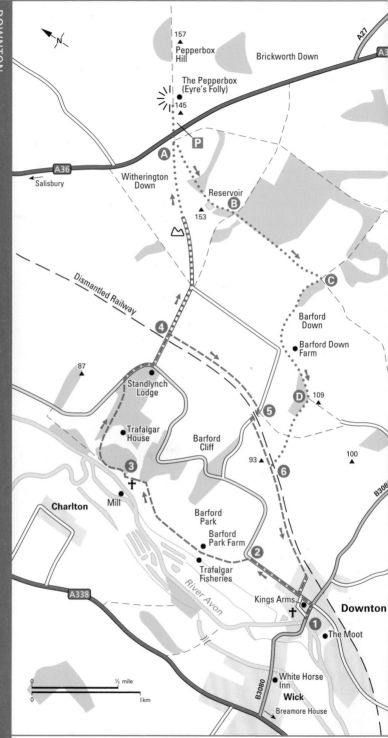

157 ▲
Pepperbox
Hill

Brickworth Down

A27

A3

The Pepperbox
(Eyre's Folly)

145

A36

A Salisbury

Witherington
Down

P

Reservoir

B

153 ▲

Dismantled Railway

C

Barford
Down

Barford Down
Farm

4

87 ▲

Standlynch
Lodge

D   109

Trafalgar
House

Barford
Cliff

5

93 ▲

100 ▲

B308

3

†
Mill

Charlton

6

Barford
Park

Barford
Park Farm

Trafalgar
Fisheries

River Avon

2

Kings Arms

†

Downton

1

The Moot

A338

0        ½ mile

0              1km

B3080

White Horse
Inn

Wick

Breamore House

① Walk up the lane between the Kings Arms and the pharmacy to the church. Turn right in front of the church along a path beside a cob wall. At the end turn left and walk along the road for about 0.5 miles (800m).

② Before the road swings right, turn left on to a track, signed to Trafalgar Fisheries. Continue on the track, between a farm and the fishery, to a cottage. Turn left here, passing the chapel on your right.

③ Where the lane bends left down to the mill, take the signed footpath, right, into the trees. Follow the main path right to a wooden gate on the woodland edge. Bear half right across a field to a metal gate (Trafalgar House is on your right), and follow the woodland path for 0.25 miles (400m) to a metalled lane. Turn right uphill, then left at the junction opposite a lodge.

④ Cross the bridge over the disused railway and take the arrowed bridle path right. Continue beside the old railway, following the right-hand edge of two fields to reach a road.

⑤ Turn right under the bridge, then left to follow the old embankment. When this peters out, maintain direction over the hill and descend to cross a track.

⑥ Descend into the valley and, as you start to ascend, take the path to the right of the embankment. At the top of the rise, turn left over a stile and continue beside the old railway. Cross a stile and keep ahead along an enclosed path to a residential road. Keep ahead for 50yds (46m) and turn right down a signposted path to a gate. Walk down the drive and turn left back to the High Street.

WHERE TO EAT AND DRINK Drop into the Kings Arms in High Street for home-made pub meals and cask ales. Alternatively, try the 15th-century White Horse Inn along The Borough.

WHAT TO SEE The crystal clear waters of the River Avon are the mainstay of the extensive and well-established organic fish farm passed on the route. Three species of trout are raised in the specially created gravel ponds – brown, rainbow and golden – both for the table and for restocking angling centres around the country. Strict environmental controls ensure that the water flowing back into this famous chalk stream is untainted.

WHILE YOU'RE THERE Venture 2 miles (3.2km) south across the border into Hampshire to visit Breamore House, a handsome Elizabethan manor house containing a fine collection of paintings, china and tapestries, acquired by 10 generations of the Hulse family.

# Pepperbox Hill

DISTANCE 7.75 miles (12.5km)    MINIMUM TIME 4hrs

ASCENT/GRADIENT 410ft (125m) ▲▲▲    LEVEL OF DIFFICULTY +++

SEE MAP AND INFORMATION PANEL FOR WALK 8

Cross the bridge over the old railway, Point ❹, and keep to the lane. At the sharp right bend, take the middle one of three tracks ahead of you. Fork right in 50yds (46m), go through a gate, and begin a long, steady climb up the track, enjoying great views towards Salisbury Cathedral. Go through a wooden gate and continue straight on over the hill. Pass a metal barrier and follow the track downhill to the A36, Point ❹. Cross the road with extreme care and follow the byway ahead, signed 'Pepperbox Hill'. Access to the folly is via the car park on your right.

Built by Giles Eyre in 1606, The Pepperbox, or Eyre's Folly, is generally regarded as one of the earliest follies in the country. It is hexagonal and brick built, with a pyramidal roof, and the windows have been bricked in on all three levels. It is believed that Eyre was envious of the towers of nearby Longford Castle and built his tower on high ground so he could overlook the castle. Some say it is not a folly at all and that Eyre built it as a hunting viewing stand.

The 24-acre (9.7ha) site on which The Pepperbox stands is one of the finest examples of chalk grassland and scrub mosaic in the county, supporting yew woodland, hawthorn and privet thickets, and juniper. The open areas and glades attract the orange clearwing moth, brimstone and grizzled skipper butterflies, while the colourful grassland in summer supports horseshoe vetch, birdsfoot trefoil, bee orchids and wild thyme.

Retrace your steps across the main road, return to the barrier gate and fork left along a grassy track. Walk past an aerial and covered reservoir and head downhill on a gravel track beside woodland. At a T-junction, Point ❸, turn left then almost immediately right, down another track. Pass a barrier gate. At a fork, bear right and continue within the edge of the woodland. This soon becomes a track between fields.

At the crossing of tracks, Point ❻, turn right and just before reaching a metalled lane, take the track left waymarked 'Restricted byway'. Walk past Barford Down Farm and ascend the grassy track which soon passes through woodland into a field. Keep left, pass a gate and in 75yds (69m) bear right across the brow of Barford Down, Point ❹, on an indistinct path. Descend across a bridleway and though a gap in the hedge; then, in 400yds (366m), turn left at the crossing of paths and join Walk 8 at Point ❻ to return to Downton.

# Vale of Pewsey and Oare Hill

DISTANCE 5 miles (8km)    MINIMUM TIME 2hrs 15min

ASCENT/GRADIENT 393ft (120m) ▲▲▲    LEVEL OF DIFFICULTY ✚✚✚

PATHS Tow paths, tracks, field paths, lanes

LANDSCAPE Vale of Pewsey and chalk downland

SUGGESTED MAP OS Explorer 157 Marlborough & Savernake Forest

START/FINISH Grid reference: SU157610

DOG FRIENDLINESS Let off lead along tow path

PARKING Fee-paying car park at Pewsey Wharf

PUBLIC TOILETS None on route

The Vale of Pewsey separates Wiltshire's two principal areas of chalk downland, Salisbury Plain to the south and the Marlborough Downs to the north. Through its heart meanders the Kennet and Avon Canal, which flows into the Thames at Reading, with the River Avon at Bath. It was used to carry iron, coal, stone and timber from Bristol and to bring luxuries like tobacco and spirits from London.

## THE GIANT'S GRAVE

The canal company built the wharf at Pewsey to serve the village, but it was never a great commercial success and was eclipsed by those at nearby Burbage to the east and Honey Street to the west. It remains much as it was in the past. The main buildings consist of the wharf keeper's cottage and the two-storey warehouse, used to store goods transported by canal. Much older than this old inland waterway, but overlooking it from the north is the Giant's Grave, an ancient unchambered burial site. It is claimed that the giant will stir from his slumbers if anyone runs around the tomb seven times. Standing on the top of Oare Hill, it is a splendid vantage point with views across the Vale of Pewsey and the North Wessex Downs.

Away to the west lie the villages of Oare and Huish. You can also see the impressive combes and dry valleys etched into the downland scarp slopes away to your right. The unimproved chalk downlands along the steep escarpment of the vale and on nearby Martinsell Hill are noted for their rich chalk grassland flora and wide variety of butterflies.

## THE VERA JEANS NATURE RESERVE

Bordering the River Avon and fed by numerous springs is the Vera Jeans Nature Reserve. This wetland reserve, or fen, is a rare environment within Wiltshire and an exciting place because of its diverse wildlife.

Since the water-meadows were abandoned, the site has developed a rich flora with 14 species of sedge (a grass-like plant). Dotted among the sedge are bogbean, bog pimpernel and southern marsh orchid. An unusual sight are the belted Galloway cattle, which graze the fen to keep the coarser vegetation at bay, allowing the more delicate flowers to thrive. The wet woodland in the middle of the reserve has an understorey of huge tussock sedges and great horsetails creating a fascinating prehistoric landscape.

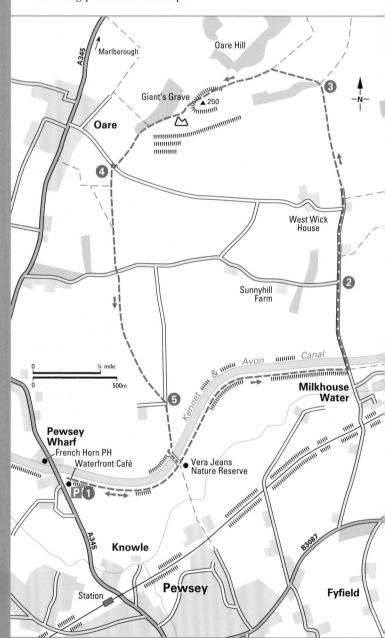

**1** Facing the canal, turn right along the tow path and walk beside the canal for just over a mile (1.6km) to the second bridge. Turn right just before it and head up to a lane. Turn left, crossing the canal bridge, and walk away from the waterway.

**2** At a road junction, keep ahead towards downland. Pass cottages on your right and proceed ahead through the gateway along the drive. When this bears left to West Wick House, continue straight on along the track, which soon narrows and begins to climb steadily towards Martinsell Hill.

**3** Go through a gate, avoid a path on the immediate left and bear left at the fork to ascend a steep sunken lane (note this can be muddy). At the top, keep left of the gate, disregard the waymarked stile on your right and bear left alongside the fence, following a path towards the long barrow on the summit of Oare Hill.

Follow the path past the trig point and descend the steep grassy slope towards Oare, soon to reach a stile at the bottom. Cross the stile, bear left along the field edge and follow the path across the field to a gate and crossing of ways.

**4** Take the footpath ahead, bearing right, then left around the field edge to reach a lane. Turn left and pass a bungalow. Continue on the lane and take the next track on the right (signposted Pewsey), heading in a southerly direction across open farmland.

**5** Keep ahead where it bears right towards a farm and continue to the Kennet and Avon Canal. Cross the bridge and bear left, passing the Vera Jeans Nature Reserve. On reaching the tow path just beyond it, turn left and retrace your steps back to the car park at Pewsey Wharf.

WHERE TO EAT AND DRINK  Occupying the former wharfinger's cottage and with its small canalside garden, the welcoming Waterfront Café at Pewsey Wharf offers light lunches and snacks all day and is the perfect resting place after you have completed your walk. Seasonal opening. Alternatively, try the French Horn pub across the bridge.

WHAT TO SEE  From the Giant's Grave, look west across Oare to locate Oare House on the west side of the village. This small mansion has associations with Clough Williams-Ellis of Portmeirion fame. He added the symmetrical wings in the 1920s.

WHILE YOU'RE THERE  Cut into Pewsey Hill south of the village is the Pewsey White Horse, carved in 1937 on the site of an older horse (1785) to celebrate the coronation of George VI. The climb is worth it for the inspiring views.

# Salisbury's Historic Trail

| | |
|---|---|
| DISTANCE 3 miles (4.8km) | MINIMUM TIME 2hrs |

ASCENT/GRADIENT Negligible ▲▲▲     LEVEL OF DIFFICULTY ✦✦✦

PATHS Pavements and metalled footpaths

LANDSCAPE City streets and water-meadows

SUGGESTED MAP OS Explorer 130 Salisbury & Stonehenge; AA Street by Street Salisbury

START/FINISH Grid reference: SU141303

DOG FRIENDLINESS Not suitable for dogs

PARKING Central car park (signed off A36 Ring Road)

PUBLIC TOILETS Central car park, Market Place, Crane Bridge Road

Salisbury, or New Sarum, founded in 1220 following the abandonment of Old Sarum and built at the confluence of four rivers, is one of the most beautiful cathedral cities in Britain. Relatively free from sprawling suburbs and high-rise development, the surrounding countryside comes in to meet the city streets along the river valleys. Throughout the city centre, buildings of all styles blend harmoniously, from the 13th-century Bishop's Palace in The Close, the medieval gabled houses and historic inns and market places to stately pedimented Georgian houses and even the modern shopping centre.

## MAJESTIC CATHEDRAL AND CLOSE

Salisbury's skyline is dominated by the magnificent spire of the cathedral, a graceful centrepiece to the unified city. An architectural masterpiece, built in just 38 years during the 13th century, the cathedral is unique for its uniformity of style. The tower and spire, with a combined height of 404ft (123m) – the tallest in England – were added in 1334, and the west front of the building is lavishly decorated with row upon row of beautifully carved statues in niches. The rich and spacious interior contains huge graceful columns of Purbeck stone, and many windows add to the airy, dignified interior. Of particular interest are the impressive tombs and effigies in the nave, the cloisters and the library, home to a copy of the Magna Carta.

The Cathedral Close is one of the largest and finest in Britain. It is entered by a series of medieval gateways and contains several grand structures in a rich variety of architectural styles, dating from the 13th century to the present day. Four of these fine buildings are open to the public as museums. The highlights are probably Malmesbury House, originally a 13th-century canonry, with its magnificent roccoco plasterwork and an Orangery that once sheltered Charles II, and

Mompesson House (owned by the National Trust), an exquisite Queen Anne building with period furnishings, china and paintings.

## CITY STREETS

You can wander through a fascinating network of medieval streets and alleys, with names like Fish Row, Silver Street and Ox Row, lined with half-timbered and jettied houses. You will see 15th-century St Thomas's church, noted for its *Doom* painting (c.1475), believed to be the largest painting of the Last Judgement in existence; the hexagonally buttressed 15th-century Poultry Cross, the last of four market crosses in the city; the timbered medieval house of John A'Port (Crew Clothing Co) in Queen Street; and the Joiners' Hall with its superb Jacobean facade in St Ann Street.

Away from the hustle and bustle, your riverside stroll through Queen Elizabeth's Gardens and along the Town Path to Harnham Mill will reveal the famous view across the water-meadows to the cathedral, much admired by many an artist.

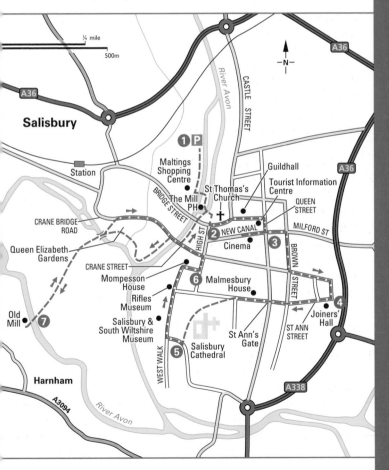

*Overleaf: Stonework on the facade of Salisbury Cathedral (Walk 11)*

**1** Join the Riverside Walk and follow the signposted path through the Maltings Shopping Centre towards St Thomas's Church. On reaching St Thomas's Square, with Cote Brasserie on your left, bear right to the junction of Bridge Street, Silver Street and the High Street.

**2** Turn left along Silver Street and cross the road to the Poultry Cross. Keep ahead along Butcher Row and Fish Row to pass the Guildhall and tourist information centre. Turn right along Queen Street, then turn right along New Canal to view the cinema foyer.

**3** Return to the crossroads and continue ahead along Milford Street to pass the Red Lion. Turn right along Brown Street, then left along Trinity Street to pass Trinity Hospital. Pass Love Lane into Barnard Street and follow the road right (Dolphin Street) to reach St Ann Street, almost opposite the Joiners' Hall.

**4** Walk down St Ann Street and keep ahead on merging with Brown Street to reach the T-junction with St John's Street. Cross straight over and go through St Ann's Gate into the Cathedral Close. Pass Malmesbury House and Bishops Walk and take the path diagonally left across the green to reach the main entrance to the cathedral.

**5** Pass the entrance, walk beside the barrier ahead and turn right. Shortly, turn right again along West Walk, passing the Salisbury and South Wiltshire Museum and the Rifles Museum. Keep ahead around Chorister Green to pass Mompesson House.

**6** Bear left through the gates into High Street and turn left at the crossroads along Crane Street. Cross the River Avon and turn left along the metalled path beside the river through Queen Elizabeth Gardens. Keep left by the play area and cross two footbridges to follow the Town Path across the water-meadows to the Old Mill (hotel) in Harnham.

**7** Return along Town Path, cross the footbridge and keep ahead to Crane Bridge Road. Bear right, recross the River Avon and turn immediately left along the riverside path to Bridge Street. Cross straight over and follow the path ahead towards The Mill. Walk back through the Maltings Shopping Centre to the car park.

**WHERE TO EAT AND DRINK** Old pubs, tea rooms and restaurants abound around the cathedral and its close. Try The Mill, an 18th-century riverside pub in The Maltings, Reeve coffee shop and tea room in the Market Place, or the historic Haunch of Venison in Minster Street. Enjoy a civilised afternoon tea in the garden of Mompesson House in The Close.

**WHAT TO SEE** Go into the foyer of the cinema in New Canal to view John Halle's 15th-century banqueting hall. Composer George Frideric Handel is thought to have given his first concert in England in the room above St Ann's Gate. While in the cathedral, look out for the 14th-century clock, believed to be the oldest working clock in the world.

**WHILE YOU'RE THERE** Discover more about Salisbury's fascinating history by visiting the award-winning Salisbury and South Wiltshire Museum, housed in the 14th-century King's House within The Close. Climb the steps up the cathedral tower for a splendid bird's-eye view across the city and the surrounding countryside.

# Lydiard Park

DISTANCE 2.5 miles (4km)    MINIMUM TIME 1hr

ASCENT/GRADIENT 65ft (20m) ▲▲▲    LEVEL OF DIFFICULTY ✦✦✦

PATHS Well-defined parkland paths and tracks, one stretch of quiet road

LANDSCAPE Farmland, parkland, woodland

SUGGESTED MAP AA Leisure Map 15 Swindon & Devizes

START/FINISH Grid reference: SU101844

DOG FRIENDLINESS Can be off lead in country park

PARKING Free parking at Lydiard Country Park

PUBLIC TOILETS Lydiard Country Park

Right on the edge of the modern town of Swindon lies the 244-acre (99ha) Lydiard Park, an easily accessible and delightful buffer against any further westward urban spread. Within the wooded and eminently explorable park is one of Wiltshire's smaller and lesser known stately homes, a Palladian mansion, the ancestral home of the Viscounts Bolingbroke, and their church, St Mary's, in the village of Lydiard Tregoze. This walk takes you through the park to the edge of the sleepy hamlet of Hook Street, following signposted paths and tracks.

## LYDIARD HOUSE AND PARK

The present house, built in 1743, was saved from dereliction by the Swindon Corporation in 1943. Part of the property now serves as a hostel, but the ground floor has been restored to its former 19th-century glory, complete with ornate plasterwork, original family furnishings, a rare painted glass window, portraits of the St John family (the Bolingbrokes) who lived here from Elizabethan times, and lifelike waxwork inhabitants. As one of Wiltshire's smaller stately homes, it has an intimate atmosphere rarely found in larger houses that have opened their doors to the public. Here you have the impression of stepping back in time to pay a social call on wealthy relations, a family, which like many of us, has had its share of ups and downs. Even the park has had its misfortunes; it was used as a prisoner of war camp at the end of World War II, and later lost all the fine elm trees, which lined the driveway from 1911, to Dutch elm disease.

## THE BOLINGBROKE FAMILY

During the Civil War the Bolingbrokes sided with the losing Royalists and although rewarded during the Restoration were disappointed when Henry St John (1652–1742) was bestowed with the title of a 'mere' Viscount in 1712 rather than becoming an Earl. Rather too close a friendship with France in the early 18th century led to a period of exile for Henry before he received a royal pardon. In 1768 the Second Viscount, Frederick St John, sensationally for the time, divorced his wife, Lady Diana Spencer, daughter of the Duke of Marlborough. Further periods of 'absenteeism', this time to Germany, and heavy mortgage liabilities finally saw the break-up of the estate in the 1920s and 1930s.

## ST MARY'S CHURCH

The church contains a further history of the family in the form of memorials. Family trees, paintings, stained-glass windows and tomb effigies are all in evidence. The most impressive of the latter is The Golden Cavalier, a magnificent, life-size, fully gilded statue of Sir John St John (1585–1648). He emerges from his tent fully clad for one of the Civil War battles. As imposing as he looks one cannot but think of the inner sadness of a man who in that conflict lost his King and three of his sons.

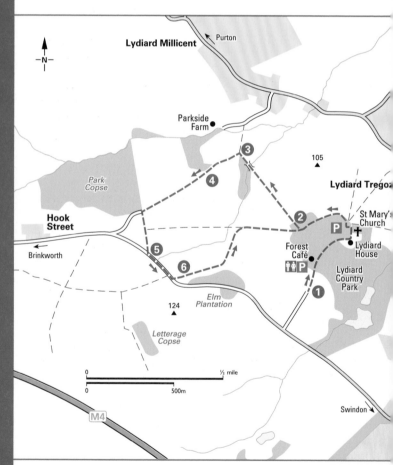

**1** Turn left out of the car park, pass the Forest Café and continue along the track to Lydiard House and the church. With the church on your right, bear left through the car park, ignoring the gate on your right, and go through another gate. Walk beside a walled garden and follow the path ahead, curving left into woodland.

**2** Just before reaching a small clearing, turn right signposted Lydiard Millicent and Purton to reach a gate on the woodland edge. Proceed straight ahead across the field on a defined path to a bridge spanning a stream.

**3** Pass beneath electricity cables and turn left at a junction signposted 'West Park Circuit'. Follow the straight path with plantations to the right and, at the next junction, with a path to Lydiard Millicent on the right, turn left on the path marked 'West Park Circuit'.

**4** Keep woodland on the right and follow a track. Go through gates and continue ahead, avoiding a left-hand path back to Lydiard House on the left. Keep ahead with hedgerow and trees to your right and at the next field corner bear right to the road at Hook Street.

**5** Turn left, follow the narrow lane between fields and trees, pass under cables again and avoid a stile and footpath on the right. Turn left a few paces beyond it, through a galvanised kissing gate.

**6** Bear right, following the field-edge alongside trees. Go through a gateway, turn immediately left and follow a grassy path alongside fencing. Bear right on reaching a clearly defined track, with Lydiard House seen ahead framed by trees. Head for the clearing and retrace your steps back to the country park and car park.

WHERE TO EAT AND DRINK  Seek refreshment in the Forest Café within the park's visitor centre, or the Coach House tea rooms in the grounds. The Sun at Lydiard Millicent is a short drive away. Alternatively, picnic beneath shady trees on the lawn in front of Lydiard House.

WHAT TO SEE  Look out for the ice house, which supplied ice to the Lydiard kitchens, and the 18th-century Ha Ha, a steep-sided, brick-lined trench, which kept cattle and sheep out of the park. In St Mary's Church look for the 15th-century wall paintings and the splendid 17th-century St John Triptych, a monument of painted display panels commemorating the St John family.

WHILE YOU'RE THERE  Near by, in Swindon, you'll find Steam – Museum of the Great Western Railway, where you will discover the remarkable story of the railway by means of various imaginative and fascinating exhibits. At Blunsdon Station, near Purton, is the Swindon and Cricklade Railway, Wiltshire's only standard-gauge heritage railway, which operates both steam and diesel locomotives.

# Grovely Wood from Great Wishford

| | |
|---|---|
| DISTANCE 5 miles (8km) | MINIMUM TIME 2hrs 30min |

ASCENT/GRADIENT 370ft (113m) ▲▲▲     LEVEL OF DIFFICULTY ✚✚✚

PATHS Woodland paths and downland tracks

LANDSCAPE Chalk downland, wooded hillside and lush water-meadow

SUGGESTED MAP OS Explorer 130 Salisbury & Stonehenge

START/FINISH Grid reference: SU080353

DOG FRIENDLINESS Can be off lead through Grovely Wood and on high downs

PARKING Roadside parking in South Street, Great Wishford

PUBLIC TOILETS None on route

Great Wishford is the most southerly of a series of villages in the valley of the River Wylye, which gives its name to Wilton and so to the county of Wiltshire. Our knowledge of the village pre-dates the Norman conquest (1066), the written name changing over the years from Wicheford or Witford to Willesford Magna in the mid-16th century and Wishford Magna by the early 17th century. Many of the village houses are constructed of Chilmark stone, quarried in the next valley. Some are interlaced with flint, others are thatched.

## 'GROVELY AND ALL GROVELY'

Oak Apple Day, 29 May, the only ancient custom still taking place in the county, commemorates the villagers' victory over the Earl of Pembroke, who, in creating Wilton Park closed the east–west road, south of the River Nadder, thus interfering with their ancient rights to cut and gather timber in the nearby Grovely Wood. Celebrations begin at dawn when the young people of the village wake each household by banging tin pans and shouting 'Grovely, Grovely, Grovely and All Grovely'. Armed with billhooks and accompanied by traditional musicians they walk up Grovely Lane into the woods, where they cut green branches for their houses and an oak bough, which is decked with ribbons and hung from the church tower. Led by the parish rector, villagers dressed in period costume then go on to Salisbury Cathedral where further celebrations, in the form of dancing on the cathedral green and a procession to the high altar, culminate in the villagers proclaiming their rights and chanting 'Grovely! Grovely! and All Grovely! Unity is strength'.

These unusual village celebrations seem to date back to a pagan and primitive period when tree worship was connected with May Day celebrations. It is interesting to note that the village has been in the ownership of just three families over the last seven centuries.

## BREAD STONES

An unusual feature in the village are the stone inscriptions that can be found in the east wall of the churchyard. These tablets record the price of bread in the village since the Napoleonic Wars. In 1801 it was 3s 10d a gallon, in 1904 only 10d and by 1920 it had risen to 2s 8d. The 'Gall' measures are a reminder of the days when bread was sold in semi-liquid form as dough for home-baking.

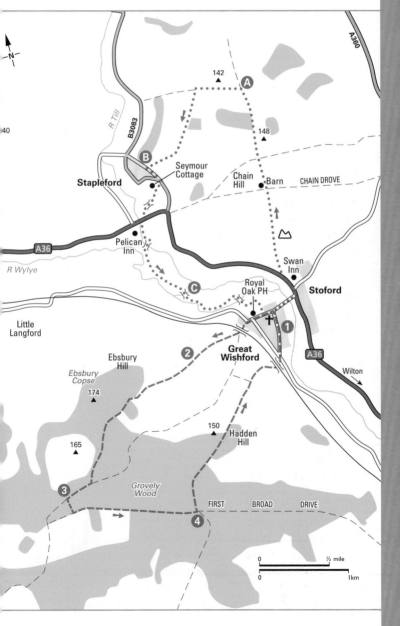

**1** Head along South Street to the church and turn left at the T-junction. Walk past the Royal Oak. Go under the railway bridge and immediately turn right to walk along the waymarked bridle path beside a cemetery. Ascend the track to a bench and gate.

**2** Go through, walk along the left-hand field-edge to a gate, continue beside trees and follow the bridleway ahead, bearing right around the top of the field and making for the opening that leads into woodland (blue waymarker). Turn almost immediately left along the woodland track, following it for some distance to a T-junction. Turn right up the metalled lane.

**3** At the first major junction, by a patch of grass, turn left and then left again to follow a track running down a broad beech avenue (First Broad Drive) along the course of a Roman road, or Lead Road, which traversed Wessex from the lead mines of the Mendips in Somerset to join other ancient routes at Old Sarum, such as the Harrow Way to Kent. You are now walking through Grovely Wood, a fine stretch of woodland that was once a royal hunting forest and which, together with the New Forest and Cranborne Chase, formed a very significant preserve.

**4** Ignore several forestry tracks, but after a mile (1.6km), at a crossing of public bridle paths (the sign is to the left, behind you), turn left and keep to the main track downhill through the woodland, ignoring all cross paths and forks. Emerge from Grovely Wood and follow the track downhill towards Great Wishford. Pass beneath the railway line to the lane. Turn left, then fork right along South Street.

**WHERE TO EAT AND DRINK** Local ales and traditional pub meals, including a Sunday carvery, are served in the creeper-clad Royal Oak in Great Wishford. Alternatively, try the Swan Inn at Stoford or the Pelican Inn at Stapleford – both offer pub food and have riverside gardens.

**WHAT TO SEE** Spend time in the Church of St Giles in Great Wishford. Note the tombs of two old village families, the Bonhams and Grobhams, and the parish fire engine, one of the earliest ever built. Made entirely of wood by Richard Newsham in 1728, it could provide 65 gallons (295 litres) of water and cost the churchwardens £33 3s 0d. Surprisingly, it was last used as recently as the mid-1920s to fight a blaze in the village.

**WHILE YOU'RE THERE** Nearby Wilton, the former capital of Saxon Wessex, offers plenty of interest. Wilton House, home to the Earls of Pembroke, is a splendid 17th-century mansion boasting a famous art collection, fine furniture and 21 acres (8.5ha) of landscaped parkland. Explore the town's museum and, if time allows, visit the impressive Italian-style Church of St Mary and St Nicholas.

# Till and Wylye Valleys

DISTANCE 4.5 miles (7.2km)    MINIMUM TIME 2hrs 15min

ASCENT/GRADIENT 278ft (85m) ▲▲▲    LEVEL OF DIFFICULTY ✚✚✚

SEE MAP AND INFORMATION PANEL FOR WALK 13

Unlike many of the chalk downland valleys across the Salisbury Plain, the valley of the River Till is the only one with a permanent flow of water. Numerous springs high up in the heart of the plain continuously feed the little river, which rises near Tilshead and flows south to merge with the much larger River Wylye at Stapleford.

Walk to the T-junction by the church and turn right along West Street, crossing the river to the A36. Turn left, cross the road just past the Swan Inn and fork right uphill along a track. Climb through trees and continue between fields. Keep straight on over Chain Drove, by a barn, and the next crossing of byways. Pass a copse and soon take the track left, Point Ⓐ. Follow this track as it bears sharp left, then heads downhill and veers right, eventually reaching a lane in Stapleford, Point Ⓑ.

There are seven other Staplefords in England, for Stapleford is the name given by the Saxons to a common feature of 'a ford marked by a post or staple' which would probably serve to indicate the shallowest place in the stream. In Wiltshire it became the name of a strategic point where

the ancient road from Old Sarum to Bath crosses the Till. There are four distinct parts of the village – Uppington, Church Street, Overstreet (or 'the settlement opposite') which lies clustered beside a castle mound dating from the 12th century, and Serrington beside the A36.

Turn left, then reach the B3083. Cross straight over on to a bridle path. Turn left along a walled path before Seymour Cottage, then keep right between fences, cross a footbridge and soon go through a gate to the A36. Cross over, turn right, then left along the footpath before the bridge. Cross a stile, follow the right-hand field-edge to a stile and plank bridges, then cross a field and turn left alongside the River Wylye to a footbridge, Point Ⓒ.

Keep the river to your right, crossing more stiles and footbridges. In 100yds (91m) beyond a thatched cottage, climb the stile on your right, then cross a footbridge and further stile before turning left towards farm buildings. Go through a wooden gate, turn right up the drive to the lane and turn left back to the church and South Street.

# Sarsen Stones on Fyfield Down

| | |
|---|---|
| DISTANCE 6 miles (9.7km) | MINIMUM TIME 2hrs 30min |

ASCENT/GRADIENT 328ft (100m) ▲▲▲     LEVEL OF DIFFICULTY ✚✚✚

PATHS Downland tracks and field paths

LANDSCAPE Lofty downland pasture and gallops

SUGGESTED MAP AA Leisure Map 15 Swindon & Devizes

START/FINISH Grid reference: SU159699

DOG FRIENDLINESS Lead required for conservation areas and around livestock

PARKING Car park at end of road leading to Manton House (north of A4, west of Marlborough)

PUBLIC TOILETS None on route

NOTES Racehorses in training may be encountered on this walk, between dawn and noon

A feature of Fyfield Down and neighbouring Overton Down are the sarsen stones that litter this intriguing chalk limestone landscape. Sarsens are natural deposits of extremely hard siliceous sandstone that derive from Tertiary deposits, later eroded and moved by glaciation some 25 million years ago. Although found elsewhere, they are not on the scale seen in the Marlborough district. Sarsens are also known as 'druid stones' or 'grey wethers', the latter due to their resemblance at a distance to a flock of sheep, the word 'wether' coming from the Old English for sheep.

Sarsens have been of great importance to humans since prehistoric times. The hard flints were used to make hand axes and other useful tools during the Bronze Age. From the 5th century AD to the mid-19th century, sarsens were used for building stone, constructing the nearby villages of West Overton and Lockeridge, gateposts, and as paving stones and tramway setts. More importantly, Fyfield Down was the stone quarry supplying Avebury stone circle and possibly Stonehenge. Stones weighing as much as 40 tons were dug up, sometimes shaped, and dragged over the downs by hundreds of people pulling them on wooden rollers with woven grass ropes.

In 1956 Fyfield Down was declared a National Nature Reserve, to protect this fine stretch of natural downland and Britain's best assemblage of sarsen stones, which support nationally important lichens, and preserve the extensive prehistoric field systems here.

## ANCIENT BYWAYS

Two historic trackways are encountered on this downland circuit. The first, the Herepath, is an ancient east–west route across the Marlborough Downs. The name is derived from the Old English word 'here' meaning an army or multitude. It suggests that this may have been one of the defensive routes established by King Alfred in the 9th century AD in his struggle with the Danes. Today it forms part of the Wessex Ridgeway route, which crosses our circuit at points ❸ and ❺.

The Ridgeway is an ancient highway incorporating a complicated network of green lanes, and follows a natural route on high ground. It was used as a drove road or trading route and served as a convenient means for invaders, peaceful or warlike, to penetrate the heartland of southern England before Anglo-Saxon times. The 87-mile (140km) Ridgeway National Trail forms only part of the route, although by linking several trails you can walk the entire route up through Oxfordshire and into Buckinghamshire.

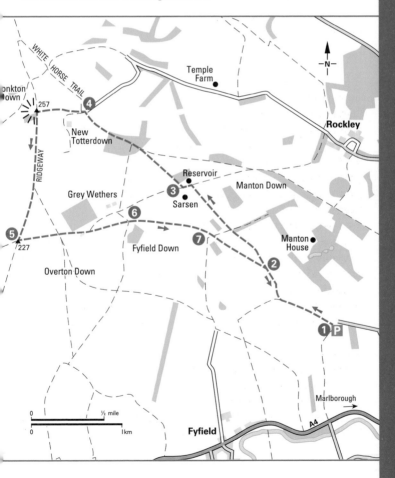

**1** Leave the car park by the track in the top right-hand corner, signposted 'White Horse Trail to Avebury and Hackpen'. Follow the track right and shortly fork left, continuing between high hedges.

**2** Pass a private road to Manton House on the right. Stay on the gently rising track and continue straight on between the gallops on Clatford Down, with good views. On reaching a T-junction by a covered reservoir, turn left along the Herepath (Green Street).

**3** Shortly, turn right through a gate waymarked 'Hackpen', to join a grassy track alongside a conifer plantation, then head across pasture to a gate into conservation woodland. Follow the track (can be muddy) through the sparse woodland, passing a Natural England signboard in the middle. Reach the edge of the wood, cross over a track and keep straight ahead between hedges along the right-hand field-edge.

**4** At a crossing of tracks, turn left through a gate by a cattle grid and walk parallel to the track. Keep to the right of gates ahead, and follow the grassy track straight ahead. Cross a gallop via two gates and reach the Ridgeway track, with views to the tumuli on Monkton Down to your right. Turn left and follow the rutted track along the escarpment and gently downhill for 0.75 miles (1.2km), enjoying extensive views to the west.

**5** At the crossways by an information board, turn left to go through a gate and on to Fyfield Down. Proceed along a grassy track and cross a gallop via three gates. This is prime racehorse-training country and there are many racing stables in the area. Continue to the right of a wood, then in the valley bottom, fork right off the gravel track and ascend a grassy track, passing more sarsen stones.

**6** At the top, go through a gate at the corner of a wooded enclosure and turn right along the field-edge. Pass through a gate in the bottom corner and continue straight on across grassland on a defined track. Pass a redundant gate, then follow the curving path round to the right over a further gallop to a furlong pole at the end of a line of trees. Swing left over a broad green gallop to a waymarker post beside a standing sarsen.

**7** Bear half right diagonally across two broad gallops, and go through the gap in the hedge to reach the track. Turn right and follow the outward route back to the car park.

**WHERE TO EAT AND DRINK** There are no refreshment places along the route of this walk but, if you bring your own, the Ridgeway track with its far-reaching views provides the perfect picnic spot. Nearby Manton and Lockeridge have pubs, while Marlborough offers the full range of refreshment facilities.

**WHAT TO SEE** As you stride across this rock-strewn landscape, note the chequerboard appearance of the field systems. Banks or 'lynchets' some 8ft (2.4m) high have formed where sarsens had been moved to create field boundaries, arresting soil movement caused by ploughing over the centuries.

**WHILE YOU'RE THERE** Visit Avebury (see walks 18 and 19) to view the largest stone circle in Europe and explore the Alexander Keiller Museum to learn more about the prehistoric archaeology of this area.

# Historic Old Sarum

DISTANCE 6.25 miles (10.1km)   MINIMUM TIME 2hrs 30min

ASCENT/GRADIENT 557ft (170m) ▲▲▲   LEVEL OF DIFFICULTY ✛✛✛

PATHS Footpaths, tracks, bridle paths, stretches of road, several stiles

LANDSCAPE Downland, river valley, castle ramparts

SUGGESTED MAP OS Explorer 130 Salisbury & Stonehenge

START/FINISH Grid reference: SU139326

DOG FRIENDLINESS Keep dogs on lead at all times

PARKING Old Sarum car park (English Heritage); closes 6pm, 3–4pm winter

PUBLIC TOILETS Old Sarum car park (free)

Set on a bleak hill overlooking modern-day Salisbury (New Sarum) stand the massive, deserted ramparts and earthworks of the original settlement of Old Sarum. People have lived here for some 5,000 years – the outer banks and ditches were constructed during the Iron Age to create a huge hill-fort. It was later inhabited by the Romans and several Roman roads converge on the site. The Saxons followed and developed a town within the prehistoric ramparts.

## THE RISE OF CHRISTIANITY

Soon after the Conquest, the Norman invaders realised the camp's strength and built the inner earthworks. Within the massive hilltop defences they built a royal castle, two palaces and, in 1075, Bishop Osmund constructed the first cathedral. Osmund's cathedral set new standards which were widely adopted in other English cathedrals. Instead of being run on monastic lines, it was served by 36 canons living in separate lodgings under the direction of four officers. The architecture was Romanesque and characterised by its lavish scale. Following Osmund's death in 1099, Bishop Roger was responsible for the ambitious rebuilding of the cathedral soon after 1100.

Old Sarum rapidly developed and for 150 years it thrived. As the cathedral grew more powerful, friction developed between the clergy and the military governor of the castle at Old Sarum. After Roger's death in 1139, the city went into decline and quarrelling increased between the two powers. The vitality and wealth of the Church, combined with the exposed site, lack of space to expand the cathedral and the shortage of water at Old Sarum, led to the removal of the cathedral to a new city by the River Avon in the early 13th century. Building work on the new cathedral began in 1220 and was largely completed by 1250.

The castle remained in use until Tudor times. Today, it is deserted and you can roam across the ramparts and ruins, admiring the Avon Valley views. A fee is charged to view the inner bailey ruins.

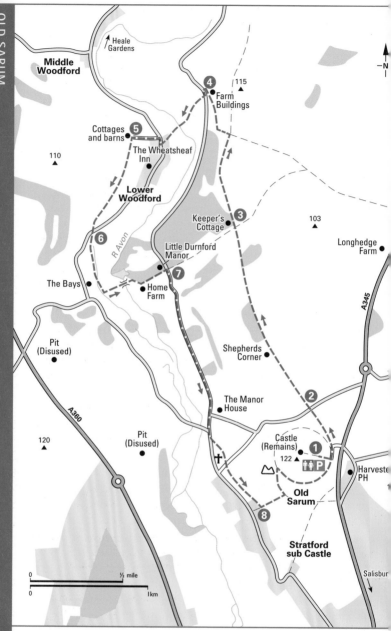

① From the car park, walk down the access road through the outer bank of the fortified site. Bear left, then, as the road bends right, go through the two gates leading to a waymarked and fenced bridle path and follow this until you reach a road.

② Go through the gate opposite and follow the track ahead. Pass a cottage (Shepherds Corner) and ascend the track. In 0.25 miles (400m), descend to Keeper's Cottage and a crossing of paths.

**3** Keep straight on, heading uphill and between fields into a wooded area. At a crossing of bridle paths, turn left and descend a tree-lined path. Follow the path down to farm buildings and continue to a road.

**4** Turn left, then right in 50yds (46m) down a metalled lane. Cross the River Avon and two further footbridges, then follow the metalled path and drive to a road. Turn left for The Wheatsheaf Inn; otherwise, turn right and in 50yds (46m) turn left up a lane.

**5** Just before cottages and barns, turn left through a kissing gate and walk down the left-hand field-edge. Go through another kissing gate, then ahead and over a stile. Walk on beside a hedge. At the edge of a field, by a permissive footpath, maintain direction across a field, cross a track and go straight on. Continue on this line, through a hedge gap, to meet the road on your left, by a footpath sign.

**6** Cross the road diagonally and take the path down a wooded track. Pass to the left of 'The Bays' to a stile

and turn right between the stream and fence. Cross double stiles in the corner and turn sharp left over a stile and turn right beside the stream to a small gate and a metalled drive. Turn left and skirt Home Farm and Little Durnford Manor to an electronic gate (green button on right) and road.

**7** Turn right and follow the road for 0.75 miles (1.2km) to a staggered crossroads. Keep ahead towards Salisbury, crossing the stile on your left in 100yds (91m). Bear half left across the field, then skirt the churchyard to reach a stile, a metalled path and a further stile. Head down the next field, cross a stile and keep right of a barn, then cross a stile on a fenced track.

**8** Meet a track and turn left uphill towards the tree-covered ramparts. Keep left at the junction of paths by a gate, then fork right through a gate and climb on to the outer rampart. Go through a gate, turn right and follow the path to a gate and Old Sarum's access road. Turn left back to the car park.

**WHERE TO EAT AND DRINK** Halfway through the walk, at Lower Woodford, you'll find good food and Hall & Woodhouse Dorset ales at the attractive, mellow redbrick Wheatsheaf Inn.

**WHAT TO SEE** Walk around the outer bailey at Old Sarum for stunning views of Salisbury and the surrounding countryside. There's free access to the remains of Bishop Roger's cathedral and its associated buildings, together with information panels that explain its history.

**WHILE YOU'RE THERE** Drive north through the Avon Valley and the Woodford villages, stopping off at Heale Gardens (open Feb–Sep), an 8-acre (3.2ha) riverside garden noted for its snowdrops, early spring colours and varied plant collections. Refreshments are served in the pleasant coffee shop.

# Pewsey Vale and Down

DISTANCE 10 miles (16.1km)    MINIMUM TIME 4hrs 30min

ASCENT/GRADIENT 492ft (150m) ▲▲▲    LEVEL OF DIFFICULTY +++

PATHS Tracks, field paths, tow path, metalled lanes

LANDSCAPE High downland pasture, Vale of Pewsey, village streets

SUGGESTED MAP AA Leisure Map 15 Swindon & Devizes

START/FINISH Grid reference: SU115637

DOG FRIENDLINESS Keep dogs under control across downland pasture

PARKING Tan Hill car park

PUBLIC TOILETS None on route

No one who travels in Wiltshire can fail to be impressed by the sweep of softly rounded chalk downland that rises to over 800ft (244m) above the fertile farmlands of the Vale of Pewsey. Not only are the views some of the best in Wiltshire, the land is rich in ancient settlements, frontier lines and burial sites. This walk is varied and exhilarating, encapsulating these archaeological treasures as well as exploring the vale with its meandering canal and unspoilt villages.

## WALKING WANSDYKE

The high and relatively unforested downland ridges were the prehistoric motorways. They became the boundaries between clans and kingdoms. For the defence of one in post-Roman times, the massive bank and ditch of the Wansdyke was built, visible for miles around. At least two major Saxon battles were fought along its length, one in AD 592 by the Neolithic long barrow known as Adam's Grave. In more peaceful times the Wansdyke became a natural road for drovers bringing their animals to the great stock fairs at Tan Hill. Saxon settlers were attracted by the springs and pastureland in the valley, and villages were established, although the twin villages of Alton Barnes and Alton Priors seem scarcely large enough to make one village. Nonetheless, each had its own church, linked by a sarsen stone footpath. Next upon the scene were the navvies and bargees when the Kennet and Avon Canal was built between 1794 and 1810. The benefits were short lived when Brunel's railway from London to Bristol opened in 1841.

## ALTON BARNES WHITE HORSE

Wiltshire is famous for its chalk figures in honour of the horse, though the one on Milk Hill above Alton Barnes is relatively recent. Created in 1812, it is noted for the fact that the journeyman artist absconded with the £20 fee before completing the task. He was subsequently caught and hung for his crime!

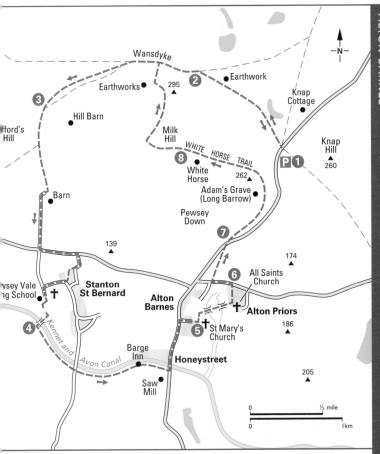

① From the car park, cross the road to a gate and follow the grassy track along the left-hand field-edge to a gate. Ascend to another gate, continue uphill and soon descend through earthworks to a T-junction with the Wansdyke.

② Turn left and continue with earthworks on your left. Begin to descend, continue ahead, cross a wooden barrier, then go through a gate and bear left off the Wansdyke on to a metalled track. Just after the track becomes concrete, fork right through a gate and follow the grassy track downhill to a gate.

③ Rejoin the main track by a barn and continue on the track. Pass more barns (on the left) and continue down to the road. Ignore the road opposite signed to Stanton St Bernard. Turn left and walk along the road (no pavement and only small grass verge) to take the next right turning for Stanton St Bernard. After this road bends left, take a narrow path on the right between fences. Turn left at the junction to follow a metalled lane. At the T-junction, turn right and pass the church, then swing left to Pewsey Vale Riding School. Turn left opposite the Riding School reception building and follow the track to the Kennet and Avon Canal.

**4** Cross the canal bridge and bear right through a gate to join the tow path. Go under the bridge and, with the canal on your left, keep to the tow path for 1 mile (1.6km), passing the Barge Inn, and bear left up to the road at Honeystreet. Turn left over the bridge into Alton Barnes. In 550yds (500m), turn right, signed to St Mary's Church.

**5** Just before the church, turn left through a turnstile and walk down a cobbled path. Follow the path right, cross two footbridges via turnstiles then, where the path turns sharp right to All Saints Church in Alton Priors, turn left across the field to a gate. A wall topped with thatch stands to the right.

**6** Turn left along the road, then just beyond the village sign, take the footpath (signed) right up the right-hand edge of the field. When the path bends sharp left by trees, follow it towards a waymarker. At the road, turn right for 50yds (46m) and fork left up a track to a gate leading on to Pewsey Down.

**7** Follow the track ahead, parallel to the road, and gradually it sweeps to the left, heading for windswept downland. Avoid a path running in from the left and continue along the track to walk above the White Horse.

**8** Continue ahead on the White Horse Trail and follow it through a gate and on until it bends right by clumps of trees. Keep right with fields on the right and a sweeping downland combe to the left. Continue round, fork right to a stile, then cross to another stile to reach the Wansdyke. Turn immediately right and retrace your steps to the car park.

**WHERE TO EAT AND DRINK** Just over halfway through the walk you can relax beside the canal outside the Barge Inn at Honeystreet. Formerly a brewery, village store, bakery and slaughterhouse for the canal community, it offers changing real ales and hearty pub food. If you can wait, enjoy a picnic on the downland by the White Horse for mesmerising views.

**WHAT TO SEE** Beside the Kennet and Avon Canal you will notice many derelict World War II brick pill boxes. The canal was part of a lowland link in the line of defence between Margate and Bristol. Pewsey Down is an important National Nature Reserve, the herb-rich turf of unimproved grassland supporting abundant chalk-loving flora and fauna, including rarities such as orchids and gentians, and butterflies, such as the Adonis blue, brown Argus, chalkhill blue and marsh fritillary.

**WHILE YOU'RE THERE** Visit the partly Saxon Church of St Mary's in Alton Barnes, with its timbered roof, Saxon nave and engraved glass panes by Laurence Whistler. Its fascinating neighbour across the field, All Saints at Alton Priors, is now redundant, but is notable for its Perpendicular tower, 12th-century chancel arch, Jacobean stalls and box pews and tombs.

# Avebury's Stone Circle

| | |
|---|---|
| DISTANCE 5 miles (8km) | MINIMUM TIME 2hrs 30min |

ASCENT/GRADIENT 262ft (80m) ▲▲▲    LEVEL OF DIFFICULTY ✦✦✦

PATHS Tracks, field paths, some road walking

LANDSCAPE Downland pasture, water-meadows, woodland and village

SUGGESTED MAP AA Leisure Map 15 Swindon & Devizes

START/FINISH Grid reference: SU099696

DOG FRIENDLINESS Keep dogs under control across pasture and NT property

PARKING National Trust car park in Avebury

PUBLIC TOILETS Avebury

Avebury's great stone circle is one of the most important megalithic monuments in Europe and it shares its setting with a pretty village. The 200 stones (only 27 remain) were enclosed in a massive earthen rampart nearly a mile (1.6km) in circumference. One can only wonder at the skill, vision and beliefs, not to mention sheer dogged hard work, that enabled the people of that time to move huge stones for many miles to create such landscapes.

## ALEXANDER KEILLER'S VISION

Avebury today owes as much to archaeologist Alexander Keiller as to the vision of our ancient ancestors. As heir to a fortune made from marmalade, Keiller was able to indulge in his passion for archaeology. In the early 1930s he came to Avebury, which then had a thriving community within and around the 4,500-year-old circle, determined to restore it to its original glory. A large part of his fortune was spent on purchasing the land, excavating the stones, and although contentious to modern archaeologists, he re-erected fallen stones and set up concrete markers to replace those he believed were missing. Trees were cleared from the ditches and, as and when the opportunity arose, buildings within the circle were purchased and demolished. Some of the villagers left the area and others went to the new houses in nearby Avebury Truslow.

Keiller's work was curtailed by lack of funds and, after World War II, he sold the site to the National Trust. His dreams were never fully realised and questions were raised as to whether he should have tried to restore the site. Should ancient landscapes be protected by riding roughshod over the interests of those who have subsequently come to live and work there?

Unlike at Stonehenge, you can roam freely around Avebury and this walk lets you explore some of Britain's finest prehistoric monuments. There is an imposing 1.5-mile (2.4km) avenue of standing stones from where, perhaps, ancient processions would lead down to Silbury Hill,

*Overleaf: Inside the West Kennett Long Barrow (Walk 18)*

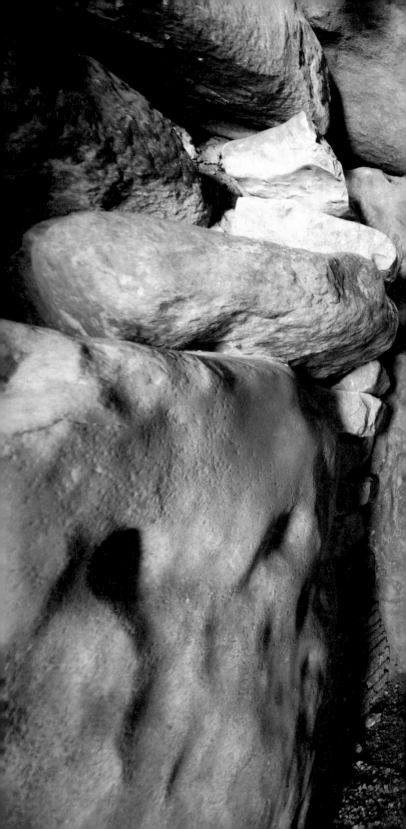

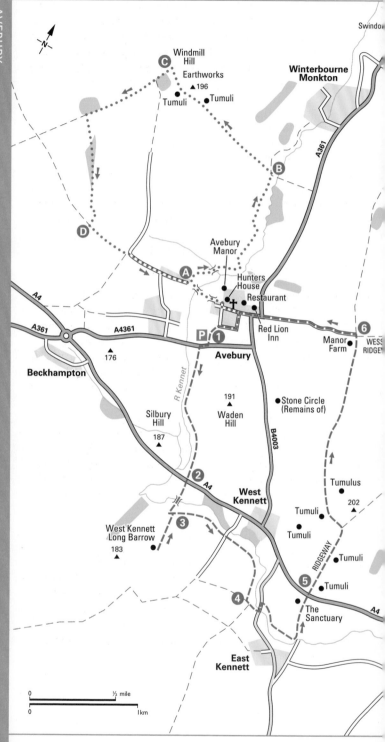

Swindo

Winterbourne
Monkton

Windmill
Hill

**C**

Earthworks

▲196

● Tumuli    ● Tumuli

A361

**B**

**D**

Avebury
Manor

Hunters
House

**A**    Restaurant

Red Lion
Inn

**6**

Manor
Farm

WESS
RIDGE

A4

A361

A4361

**P** **1**

**Avebury**

Beckhampton

▲
176

R Kennet

Stone Circle
(Remains of)

191
▲
Waden
Hill

B4003

Silbury
Hill

187
▲

**2**  A4

**West
Kennett**

Tumulus

202
▲

**3**

Tumuli

Tumuli

West Kennett
Long Barrow

183
▲

RIDGEWAY

●Tumuli

**5**   ●Tumuli

**4**

The
Sanctuary

A4

**East
Kennett**

0           ½ mile

0                      1km

an entirely artificial structure 130ft (40m) high. Smaller in scale but just as intriguing is the West Kennett Long Barrow, the second largest barrow in Britain at 300ft (91m) long. There is a liberal scattering of tumuli over the area, the last resting places of many a noble and priest. Finally, alongside the A4 is The Sanctuary, the site of major wooden buildings, possibly used for religious and burial rites.

**1** From the National Trust car park walk to the main road and turn right. In 50yds (46m), cross and go through a gateway with a blue bridleway arrow. Pass through another gate and follow the path alongside the river. Go through two more gates and cross two stiles, passing Silbury Hill.

**2** Beyond a gate, walk down the right-hand field-edge to a gate and the A4. Cross and turn left, then almost immediately right through a gate. Walk down the path and cross a bridge over a stream. Go through a kissing gate and turn sharp left.

**3** To visit West Kennett Long Barrow, shortly turn right. Otherwise go straight on around the left-hand field-edge to a stile and continue along a track. At a staggered junction, keep ahead over a stile and walk along the right-hand field boundary. Cross the stile on your right in the corner and proceed up a narrow footpath.

**4** At a T-junction, go left and descend to the road. Turn left, then just beyond the bridge, take the bridle path sharp right. Follow the right-hand field-edge to a gap in the corner and turn sharp left following a track uphill. At the top you'll see tumuli on the right and The Sanctuary on the left. Continue to the A4.

**5** Cross the A4 and head up the Ridgeway. After 500yds (457m), turn left off the Ridgeway on to a byway. Bear half right by the clump of trees on a tumulus and keep to the established track, eventually reaching a T-junction by a series of farm buildings at Manor Farm.

**6** Turn left, signed 'Avebury', and follow the metalled track through the earthwork and straight over the staggered crossroads by the Red Lion Inn. Continue along the road to the wooden signpost and walk back to the car park.

WHERE TO EAT AND DRINK Try the thatched Red Lion Inn at the heart of the stone circle for traditional pub food and atmosphere. Circle Restaurant, off the High Street, serves jacket potatoes, scones and soup, among other fare.

WHAT TO SEE Locate the huge Druid Stone, the Swindon Stone and the Barber Stone, and marvel at how they were transported and why they stay upright.

WHILE YOU'RE THERE To learn more about Keiller visit the Alexander Keiller Museum, which displays many of the exciting finds from his archaeological excavations in the area.

# Avebury and Windmill Hill

DISTANCE 4.5 miles (7.2km)   MINIMUM TIME 2hrs 15min

ASCENT/GRADIENT 131ft (40m) ▲▲▲   LEVEL OF DIFFICULTY ✦✦✦

SEE MAP AND INFORMATION PANEL FOR WALK 18

Leave the car park by the path signposted to the Rectory. At the road, turn left, walk past the church and go right opposite the Rectory. Turn left at Hunters House, walk down the drive. Tucked away behind the church is Avebury Manor. Originally a monastery, the present building dates from the early 16th century. Some of the rooms are open to the public. Outside the Manor, don't miss the exquisite flower and topiary gardens.

Cross a footbridge and a further bridge before forking right. In 50yds (46m), climb the stile on your right, Point **Ⓐ**, and proceed ahead to cross a footbridge via stiles. Bear left across the field to a stile, head straight across the next field to double stiles then maintain direction across the following large field. Negotiate three stiles at the field boundary and follow the left-hand edge of a water-meadow to a stile, Point **Ⓑ**. Turn left through a gate and ascend along the right-hand field-edge to a gate. Continue uphill to a gate on to Windmill Hill, Point **Ⓒ**.

Enclosing about 21 acres (8.5ha), Windmill Hill is one of Britain's largest neolithic causeway enclosures, consisting of three concentric ditches overlying an earlier settlement. It was a seasonal gathering place for the settlers in the Marlborough Downs area in about 3300 BC. Between the inner ditches you can see a bowl barrow and a bell barrow, which form part of a small Bronze Age burial site of about 1700–1400 BC.

Walk through the earthworks and keep to the right of a small wood. Go downhill to a gate. Turn left along the track, then fork right at the end of woodland into more open countryside. Follow the path to the left of woodland and go through the gate on the left. Follow the left field-edge, go through a gate on your left and continue along the right edge of the adjacent field. Maintain direction to a gate and along a fenced track. Bear sharp right through a gate and turn left at a junction with a track, Point **Ⓓ**.

This track becomes Bray Street, narrows to a footpath and rejoins the outward journey by the footbridges. Retrace your steps back to the car park.

*Left: Silbury Hill, near Avebury (Walk 18)*

# Barbury Castle

| | |
|---|---|
| DISTANCE 4 miles (6.4km) | MINIMUM TIME 2hrs |

ASCENT/GRADIENT 262ft (80m) ▲▲▲     LEVEL OF DIFFICULTY +++

PATHS Tracks and byways, field paths, metalled lanes

LANDSCAPE Chalk downland

SUGGESTED MAP OS Explorer 169 Cirencester & Swindon

START/FINISH Grid reference: SU156760

DOG FRIENDLINESS Let off lead in country park

PARKING Free parking at Barbury Castle Country Park

PUBLIC TOILETS Barbury Castle Country Park

Some of the finest scenery in southern England can be found on the chalk downlands of Wiltshire, in particular the Marlborough Downs, which extend south from Swindon across the Vale of Pewsey to the northern flanks of Salisbury Plain. These expansive landscapes, with their wide skies and smooth ridges interspersed with long shallow combes, have captured the imagination of many writers, including Richard Jefferies (1848–87), perhaps Wiltshire's best-known country writer. His lyrical prose was deeply influenced by the vast open downland and the far-reaching views. His favoured spot along the northern ridge of the Marlborough Downs was on Barbury Down, with its breathtaking views across the Vale of the White Horse to the Cotswolds. About 150 acres (61ha) of open land on Barbury Down have now been designated a country park.

The archaeology of the area is renowned, with a mass of ancient field monuments, including stone circles, post-Roman earthworks, field systems, burial mounds and hill-forts littering the landscape. During the Ice Age, a succession of tribes invaded Britain, many of them settling on the North Wessex Downs where they constructed dramatic hill-forts on the downland escarpments, away from the threat of advancing armies. One of the best-known hill-forts in southern England provides the focal point of the country park and this walk.

## FOLLOWING THE ANCIENT RIDGEWAY

Barbury Castle is a well-defined oval of about 12 acres (5ha), with entrances at the eastern and western sides passing through towering double ramparts, as well as ditches and other defences, which may have been added when it was re-fortified in the Saxon period. Finds from the site suggest that it was used over a long period of time and include flint axes, Iron Age and Roman pottery, weapons, tools and jewellery. You can see many of these on display in Devizes Museum. Half a mile (800m) north of the castle lies the battlefield of Beranburth, where Saxon chief Cynric and his son Ceawlin defeated the Britons in a bloody massacre. It established the Saxons as overlords of southern England and later, in AD 560, Ceawlin became King of Wessex.

The walk starts by following one of Britain's best-loved national long distance trails. Used for over 4,000 years, the Ridgeway linked East Anglia with the Dorset coast. The official route begins at Ivinghoe

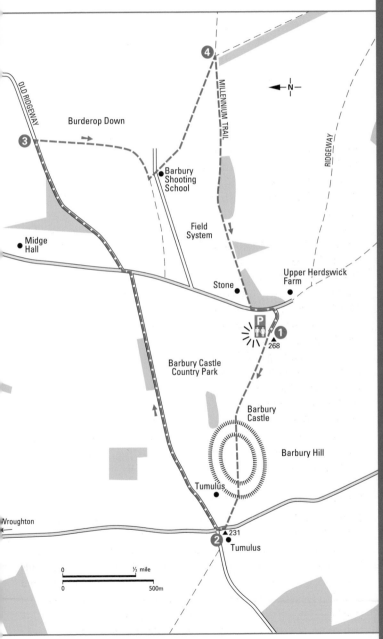

Beacon in Buckinghamshire and follows the chalk ridges to Avebury, 85 miles (137km) away.

## MEMORIAL TO A POPULAR WRITER

The walk finishes as it starts, by following another popular waymarked path – the Millennium Trail Byway. As well as offering stunning views to the north, the trail passes a memorial stone to Richard Jefferies, who was born at Coate near Swindon and spent much of his time walking the Wiltshire Downs. His plaque on the stone faces his birthplace. On the other side of the memorial stone is a plaque recalling Alfred Williams (1877–1930), self-taught scholar, linguist and nature poet, who was born at nearby South Marston.

**1** Go to the far end of the car park, passing the toilet block to reach a gate. Continue along the Ridgeway to the eastern entrance to Barbury Castle and enter the hill-fort. Walk around the rampart or straight across the centre to leave via the western entrance. Drop down the hillside to a gate. Turn right down a lane and in 50yds (46m) turn right at the crossing of ways.

**2** Follow the waymarked byway and at a T-junction turn left for 50yds (46m) along the metalled lane, then bear right at the cycle way sign (No. 45). Continue with trees on the left and then between fields to a waymarker for Barbury Castle.

**3** Turn right and follow the field-edge towards Barbury Shooting School. Pass a dilapidated barn and on reaching a waymarker on the left, at the end of a line of trees, turn left. Swing right after a few paces towards a gap in the line of trees on the brow of the hill, pass a Millennium Trail sign and continue to an angled junction.

**4** Turn sharp right, signposted 'Millennium Trail' and head for a gate. Steeply ascend Burderop Down to a stile and gate and continue to climb along the left-hand edge of a large field, past the memorial stone to Richard Jefferies and Alfred Williams. Eventually you reach a gate. Turn left up the lane and soon turn right back into the car park.

**WHERE TO EAT AND DRINK** There are no refreshment stops on the route of the walk, but plenty of pubs in the nearby villages. Alternatively, try the Honey Pot cafe in nearby Wroughton, which is open Mon–Sat 8am–3pm and offers a range of snacks and meals.

**WHAT TO SEE** As you traverse Burderop Down look for the outline of the 'Celtic' field system covering about 140 acres (57ha) of downland. Banks define the rectangular fields, which were used from the Iron Age to medieval times.

**WHILE YOU'RE THERE** Take a closer look at one of Wiltshire's eight white horse chalk figures. South along the Ridgeway path, and accessible by car via Broad Hinton, is the Hackpen White Horse, a figure 29.5yds (27m) high, cut in 1837 to celebrate Queen Victoria's coronation.

# The Infant Thames at Cricklade

| | |
|---|---|
| **DISTANCE** 5.5 miles (8.8km) | **MINIMUM TIME** 2hrs 30min |
| **ASCENT/GRADIENT** Negligible ▲▲▲ | **LEVEL OF DIFFICULTY** +++ |

**PATHS** Field paths and bridle paths, disused railway, town streets

**LANDSCAPE** Flat river valley

**SUGGESTED MAP** AA Leisure Map 15 Swindon & Devizes

**START/FINISH** Grid reference: SU100934

**DOG FRIENDLINESS** Dogs can be off lead along old railway line

**PARKING** Cricklade Town Hall car park or off Cricklade High Street beside Medical Centre (both free)

**PUBLIC TOILETS** Cricklade High Street; in car park opposite the Old Bear pub

**NOTES** North Meadow part of walk can be prone to serious flooding after heavy rain

The Thames begins life in a peaceful Gloucestershire field near Cirencester. Before long it becomes a sizeable stream – also known as the Isis at this point – on its way to the Cotswold Water Park, a vast network of lakes and pools, before reaching Cricklade. Although merely a meandering willow-fringed stream as it passes through the town, the river at Cricklade had been navigable by large barges during the 17th and 18th centuries. With the completion of the Thames and Severn Canal in 1789 though, river traffic was transferred to the canal and the upper reaches of the Thames became overgrown.

## CRICKLADE – ROMAN MILITARY POST

Cricklade's position at the junction of four ancient roads may well be why it was established as the head of the navigable Thames. However, its importance as a settlement began in Roman times when it was a significant military post on Ermine Street, the Roman road linking Cirencester and Silchester. Evidence of Roman occupation has been found in and around the town, with villas to the north and southeast. The later fortified Saxon town was built as a defence against the Danes and had its own mint. Today, the High Street has worthy buildings from the 17th and 18th centuries and two contrasting parish churches. Don't miss St Sampson's, with its cathedral-like turreted tower that rises high above the town and dominates the surrounding water-meadows.

## ABANDONED COMMUNICATION LINES

This walk follows the River Thames north, away from Cricklade, via the Thames Path. Beyond North Meadow, your route passes beside a shallow ditch that was once the North Wilts Canal, which ran the 9 miles (14.5km) between Swindon and Latton, linking the Wilts and Berks Canal with the Thames and Severn Canal. Soon you will follow the old tow path beside the muddy, weed-clogged ditch that was once the Thames and Severn Canal, opened in 1789 to link the River Severn with the Thames at Lechlade. The canal closed to all traffic in 1927, and was finally abandoned in 1933. Later the walk heads south along a disused railway line, part of the Midland and South West Railway, which was closed to passengers in 1961.

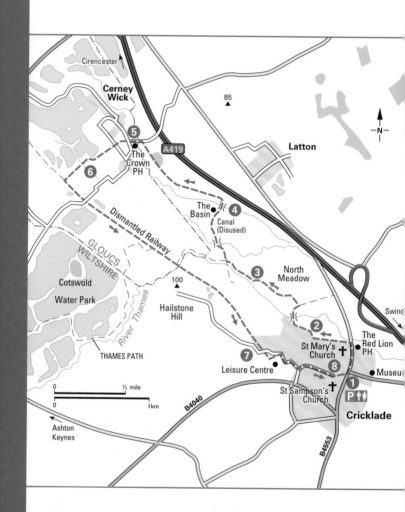

❶ Turn right out of the car park, keep ahead at the roundabout and walk along the High Street. Pass St Mary's Church, then turn left along North Wall before the river bridge. Shortly, bear right to a gate and join the Thames Path. Continue your route on the left along the field-edge to houses and go through the kissing gate. Walk along the road with houses on your left.

② Go through the kissing gate on your right and bear left across the field to a gate. Follow the fenced footpath, cross a plank bridge and pass through the gate immediately on your right-hand side. Cross the river bridge and turn left through a gate. Turn immediately right and walk up the edge of the field to the kissing gate. Cross a footbridge to enter the North Meadow. Turn left and walk parallel to the bushes on your left for 0.5 miles (800m) until the infant Thames comes into view on your left.

③ Continue on to cross a gate by a bridge. Go through another gate immediately right and keep straight ahead, ignoring the Thames Path, left. Follow the path beside the disused canal. Cross a footbridge, walking round a stile, then, at a fence, bear right to join a track and then a footbridge close to a house named The Basin. Bear right along the drive.

④ Cross a bridge and turn left through the gateway. Shortly, bear right to join the path along the left side of the old canal, keeping to the path for 0.5 miles (800m) to the road. Turn left into Cerney Wick to reach a T-junction.

⑤ Cross the stone stile opposite and keep ahead through the paddock to a stone stile and lane. Cross the lane and go through the kissing gate opposite, continuing ahead to another kissing gate and stile. Follow the path ahead. Bear right, then left and bear off down some steps on the left into trees.

⑥ Cross a footbridge with a squeeze stile and proceed ahead along the field-edge to a gate. Turn left along the old railway, signed 'Cricklade'. Cross the River Thames in a mile (1.6km), and keep to the path along the former trackbed to reach a bridge.

⑦ Go through the kissing gate and follow the gravel path to the Leisure Centre. Bear left on to the road, following it right, then turn left opposite the entrance to the Leisure Centre car park. Turn right, then next left and follow the road to the church.

⑧ Walk beside the barrier and turn right in front of The Gatehouse into the churchyard. Bear left to the main gates and follow the lane to a T-junction. Turn right to make your way back to the car park.

**WHERE TO EAT AND DRINK** You will find various pubs and hotels, notably The Red Lion near the Thames, and a traditional cafe in Cricklade. At Cerney Wick, the halfway point, The Crown offers traditional home-cooked food, real ales and a large garden.

**WHAT TO SEE** Walk across North Meadow, a National Nature Reserve, in spring to see many rare plants and flowers, including Britain's largest area of rare snakeshead fritillaries. At Cerney Wick, note the restored lock and the well-preserved roundhouse, originally the home of the lengthsman whose job was to ensure that the level of water did not drop below the necessary minimum.

**WHILE YOU'RE THERE** Visit Cricklade's small local museum where collections, photographs and maps illustrate the history of the town from the Roman era to the present day. Head for the attractive village of Ashton Keynes and the heart of the Cotswold Water Park, Britain's largest water park, with 133 lakes providing water sports, nature trails and a visitor centre at Keynes Country Park.

# Dinton and the Nadder Valley

| | | |
|---|---|---|
| DISTANCE 5.25 miles (8.4km) | MINIMUM TIME 2hrs 30min | |
| ASCENT/GRADIENT 360ft (110m) ▲▲▲ | LEVEL OF DIFFICULTY ✦✦✦ | |

PATHS Tracks, field and woodland paths, parkland, many stiles

LANDSCAPE River valley and wooded hillside

SUGGESTED MAP OS Explorer 130 Salisbury & Stonehenge

START/FINISH Grid reference: SU009315

DOG FRIENDLINESS Dogs will need to be lifted over some stiles

PARKING Dinton Park National Trust car park (free)

PUBLIC TOILETS None on route

The Nadder Valley is unlike any of the other river valleys that radiate out from Salisbury, for it is not a distinct deep valley incised in the chalk strata as is evident in the neighbouring Ebble and Wylye river valleys. This anomalous character is due to the fact that the Nadder traverses a sequence of rock types, resulting in a landscape of scarp slopes and deep combes within its broad vale. In this well-watered valley, villages free from the need to be located on the banks of the Nadder are found scattered across the landscape, nestling among lush meadows, wooded hills and along gentle tributary streams.

## FAMOUS FAMILIES

The village of Dinton is bordered by three beautifully landscaped houses, each associated with important Wiltshire families. The National Trust owns four properties here – Hyde's House, Lawes Cottage, Little Clarendon and Philipps House. The latter two are open to the public during the summer. In the old part of the village, close to St Mary's Church, is Hyde's House, an elegant building with a Queen Anne facade masking 16th-century origins. It was here that Charles II's chancellor, Edward Hyde, was born in 1609. His daughter Anne married the future James II and was mother to Queen Anne and Queen Mary.

Lawes Cottage was the 17th-century home of the Lawes family. Henry Lawes (1596–1662), a musician and composer, became Master of the King's Musick, wrote the anthem for the Coronation of Charles II and, as a friend of poet John Milton, wrote the music for his *Masque of Comus* in 1634. Next door is Little Clarendon, a Tudor manor house with a small 20th-century chapel in the garden. The grandest of all the houses is Philipps House, an imposing stone mansion with a neo-Grecian facade that dominates Dinton Park. Formerly called

Dinton House, it was completed in 1820 by Jeffrey Wyatt for William Wyndham, the last of the three great families to reside in Dinton.

Overlooking a lovely lake in peaceful parkland, Compton Park (not open to the public) was the seat of the Penruddockes, an influential Wiltshire family for 300 years from 1550. The small 13th-century church contains the family vault and the remains of John Penruddocke, a gallant gentleman who was executed in 1655 following his efforts to raise support against Parliamentarian rule.

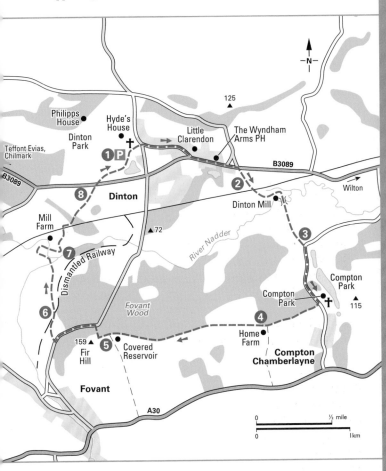

❶ Leave the car park, cross and follow the lane to the B3089. Turn left, pass the village of Little Clarendon and continue for 0.25 miles (400m), passing The Wyndham Arms. After this, take the path right opposite a junction and alongside a thatched bus shelter.

❷ Follow the track down to a kissing gate and cross the railway line to a further gate. Keep to the track and bear left alongside a stream to reach Dinton Mill. Swing right, passing in front of the mill, cross the footbridge over the River Nadder and follow the drive to a lane.

**③** Turn right and follow the metalled lane into Compton Chamberlayne. Take the footpath right, opposite the entrance to Compton Park and the church. Ascend steadily. Continue along the track to Home Farm and a junction of tracks.

**④** Turn right, follow the track left around farm buildings and remain on the track with views of the Fovant Badges. Walk beside woodland, then, on nearing the field corner, follow the narrow path into the trees and continue close to the woodland fringe. Pass a covered reservoir to reach a track.

**⑤** Turn right and walk downhill to a road. Turn left, then, at the sharp left bend, take the path acutely right and enter a field by a gap (disused stile adjacent). Bear half right over the field to a stile. Cross a tree-lined track, pass through a kissing gate and walk across rough grassland. Within 75yds (69m) move left to another kissing gate.

**⑥** Turn right along the field-edge, go through a kissing gate and bear left across the top of a field. About halfway along, turn left, downhill, to a waymarker in the lower hedge. Go through the hedge, towards Mill Farm, to a stile. Descend through scrub, cross a footbridge, then a stile and walk ahead to a further stile. Bear left along the riverbank, cross a stile and continue to a bridge over the mill stream.

**⑦** Pass in front of Mill Farm on a permissive path. Cross a footbridge and stile and bear diagonally right towards the railway. Cross the line via the underpass and bear slightly right to reach woodland and a marker post. Walk through to a stile and keep ahead, across the rear corner of a barn, to a stile. Continue ahead to a stile, then cut across pasture, between the first and second telegraph poles, to a stile and road.

**⑧** Cross the stile opposite into Dinton Park and turn right alongside the trees. Bear off left along a grassy path, pass the pond and head towards the church. Go through the first gate on your right and return to the car park.

---

**WHERE TO EAT AND DRINK** Traditional pub food and local ales can be enjoyed at the unpretentious Wyndham Arms in Dinton. The Black Dog at Chilmark (west along the B3089) is an excellent 16th-century pub with imaginative food and an informal atmosphere.

**WHAT TO SEE** Note the remarkable series of 12 regimental badges, marked 'Fovant Badges' on the OS map, etched into the chalk on Compton and Fovant downs as you walk west from Compton Chamberlayne. They were made in 1916 by men who were billeted in the area before going into action on the Western Front. Look for the gallant John Penruddocke's name on the family memorial in Compton Chamberlayne church – it states that he was 'beheaded at Exeter'.

**WHILE YOU'RE THERE** Stroll across Dinton Park and take a closer look at Philipps House (open from late March until 30 October, Mon 1–5pm, Sat 10am–1pm). You can explore the principal ground-floor rooms and learn more about the Wyndham family. Note the impressive central staircase of Portland stone and the fine views across the Nadder Valley. Drive west along the B3089 to see Teffont Evias, a charming stone village on the Teff stream.

# Old and New Wardour Castles

| | |
|---|---|
| DISTANCE 3.75 miles (6km) | MINIMUM TIME 1hr 45min |

ASCENT/GRADIENT 278ft (85m) ▲▲▲    LEVEL OF DIFFICULTY ✦✦✦

PATHS Field and woodland paths, parkland tracks, many stiles

LANDSCAPE River valley, undulating parkland

SUGGESTED MAP OS Explorer 118 Shaftesbury & Cranborne Chase

START/FINISH Grid reference: ST938264

DOG FRIENDLINESS Under control around livestock

PARKING Free parking at Old Wardour Castle

PUBLIC TOILETS Old Wardour Castle (if visiting ruin)

The ruins of Old Wardour Castle stand in a peaceful lakeside setting deep in south Wiltshire countryside. On a spur of high ground, protected by secluded woodland, they overlook the Palladian mansion of New Wardour Castle and the tranquil Nadder Valley.

## UNIQUE DESIGN

Old Wardour was constructed in 1393 for John, 5th Lord Lovel of Titchmarsh, and remodelled in 1578 by Sir Matthew Arundell. It was not built as a fortress in the familiar sense of the word but as a tower house as much for comfort as for defence. Its unusual design – hexagonal in shape and with all its rooms and chambers within the one building – is thought to have been inspired by similar structures in France, where Lord Lovel campaigned during the Hundred Years War.

## CIVIL WAR SIEGES

During the Civil War in 1643 the castle had to be defended against a Commonwealth army. A garrison of 50 soldiers and servants, along with Lady Arundell, conducted an heroic defence of Old Wardour, holding out against 1,300 of Cromwell's regulars led by Sir Edward Hungerford. Lady Arundell surrendered only when offered honourable terms, which the Roundheads immediately broke, sacking the castle and imprisoning her. Rather than destroy the castle, the Parliamentarians installed a garrison there and used it to protect themselves from a growing Royalist army in Wiltshire. Henry, Lord Arundell's son, resolved to recover his confiscated property and his home. After several unsuccessful demands for the Parliamentarians to surrender, the young Arundell lay siege to the castle in January 1644. During the siege, a gunpowder mine was laid in a drainage tunnel underneath the castle. When it exploded a large portion of the structure collapsed, leaving it uninhabitable.

## ROMANTIC RUIN

Old Wardour was never restored after the war; the Arundells built a smaller house on the south side of the bailey wall. New Wardour Castle was designed in Palladian style by James Paine for the 8th Lord Arundell and built, between 1769 and 1776, on the other side of the park. It remained the seat of the Arundell family until 1944. This fine building has since been a school, and was converted into apartments during the 1990s.

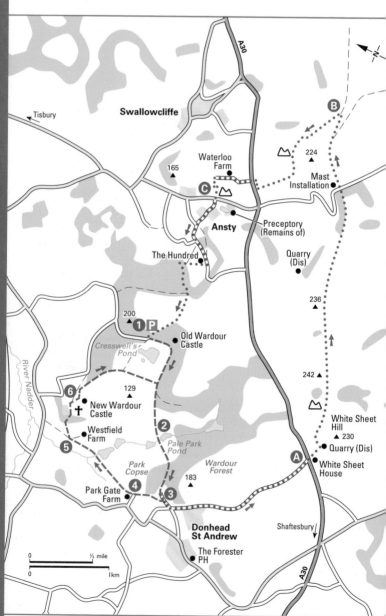

**1** From the parking area, turn left along the drive and pass between the castle and Cresswell's Pond. Pass the Gothic Pavilion, then at Wardour House (private) bear right with the trackway. Gently climb the wide track, skirting woodland, then at a fork keep right. At the end of the woodland, go through a gap into a field entrance and walk ahead along the right-hand side of the field, heading downhill to a stile.

**2** Follow the path beside Pale Park Pond to a squeeze gate, then ascend across the field to a further squeeze gate into woodland. Shortly, bear right to continue along the main forest track, before leaving Wardour Forest beside a gate on to a gravel drive.

**3** At the end of the hedge, cross the stile on your right. Head downhill across the field to a metal gate and follow the waymarked path through Park Copse, soon to bear left down a grassy clearing to a squeeze gate beside a field entrance. Follow the right-hand edge towards Park Gate Farm.

**4** Cross a stile on to the farm drive and turn right (yellow arrow) to cross the concrete farmyard to a gate.

Follow the path beside the hedge to a further gate, with the River Nadder on the left, then proceed ahead along the right-hand field-edge to a double stile in the far corner. Bear diagonally left across the field, aiming for the left-hand side of a cottage. Go through a gate and maintain direction to reach a stile.

**5** Cross the farm drive and the stile opposite and head straight uphill, keeping left of the trees, towards a stile and woodland. Follow the path right through the trees and soon bear left to pass a building on your left. New Wardour Castle is visible on your right. Following the yellow-painted post and waymarkers, keep close to the bushes across the grounds towards the main drive. Descend two steps, go ahead through a hedge and turn right.

**6** Join the drive and walk past New Wardour Castle. Where the track forks, keep right to a stile beside a gate. Follow the grassy track ahead across parkland towards Old Wardour Castle. Climb a stile beside a gate and proceed ahead, following the track uphill to a T-junction of tracks. Turn left and follow your outward route back to the car park.

WHERE TO EAT AND DRINK A short detour leads you to the appealing old thatched Forester pub in Lower Street, Donhead St Andrew, for lunchtime snacks or a full restaurant menu.

WHAT TO SEE In the grounds of Old Wardour Castle (open winter weekends, daily Apr–Sep, entrance charge), seek out the elaborate rockwork grotto and the remains of a stone circle, both part of the 18th-century landscaping improvements. Film buffs may recognise the castle as it was used extensively during the filming of *Robin Hood: Prince of Thieves* (1991).

WHILE YOU'RE THERE Visit nearby Tisbury and its magnificent 15th-century stone tithe barn, which at nearly 200ft (61m) long is reputedly the largest in England.

# White Sheet Hill and Ansty

| DISTANCE 8 miles (12.9km) | MINIMUM TIME 4hrs |
|---|---|

ASCENT/GRADIENT 787ft (240m) ▲▲▲     LEVEL OF DIFFICULTY +++

SEE MAP AND INFORMATION PANEL FOR WALK 23

Having walked to the end of the hedge, Point ❸, continue along the track to a lane and turn left through Donhead St Andrew for 1 mile (1.6km) to the A30, Point Ⓐ. Cross over and ascend the zig-zag track up White Sheet Hill. After climbing, continue for 1.5 miles (2.4km) to a road.

The ancient highway up White Sheet Hill follows the crest of chalk downland all the way to Salisbury. Centuries ago it provided dry passage for pilgrims travelling from Salisbury to the abbeys at Wilton and Shaftesbury. In later years it formed part of the coach road from the West Country to London, before the turnpike at the base of the hill.

Cross the road and soon pass a mast installation. Continue for over 0.5 miles (800m), looking for a small waymarked wooden gate on the left, just before hedgerow resumes on the right, Point Ⓑ. Turn acutely left across the field to a gate and turn left on a broad track to a further gate. Where the fence veers left, turn right steeply downhill to join a path before scrub that descends the scarp face at an angle, left. Go through two gates in the field corner and bear left across the track to go through a further gate on to a bridleway. Walk straight ahead along the field-edge to a gate and continue ahead. At the bottom, bear

right to a field gate and cross over the A30. Walk straight ahead up the drive towards Waterloo Farm. Pass between barns, join a track and take the footpath left, between hedges, just before a gate. Just a few paces after a gate on your right, take the path right and descend steeply into Ansty, Point Ⓒ.

Ansty has long been associated with royalty since Alfred and successive kings of Wessex hunted in the forests. In 1211 the manor title deeds were given to the Knights Hospitallers of the Order of St John of Jerusalem. A Preceptory was formed and they built the Church of St James, the fishpond and a hospice for pilgrims on their way to Shaftesbury Abbey.

At the lane turn left for the Preceptory or take the lane opposite. Follow it for more than 0.5 miles (800m), then take the path right, opposite a thatched house and beside The Hundred. Walk uphill towards woodland. Skirt right to cross a stile (concealed by bracken) on the woodland edge. Go ahead through the trees and bear up left on meeting a track. Turn left at a junction and follow the track to a crossing of paths. Continue ahead along a fenced path between fields. Enter woodland and descend the track ahead to the car park.

# The Ebble Valley

| | |
|---|---|
| DISTANCE 5 miles (8km)    MINIMUM TIME 2hrs 30min | |
| ASCENT/GRADIENT 377ft (115m) ▲▲▲    LEVEL OF DIFFICULTY +++ | |
| PATHS Byways, field paths, bridle paths, metalled lanes, several stiles | |
| LANDSCAPE Chalk downland and river valley | |
| SUGGESTED MAP OS Explorer 118 Shaftesbury & Cranborne Chase | |
| START/FINISH Grid reference: ST964250 | |
| DOG FRIENDLINESS Will need to be lifted over some stiles; lead required around livestock and in village streets | |
| PARKING On top of Swallowcliffe Down, where Herepath byway crosses a minor road between Ansty and Alvediston | |
| PUBLIC TOILETS None on route | |

Of all the valleys that radiate out from Salisbury, the Ebble must be the most peaceful and unspoilt. Time seems to have passed by the valley and its string of tranquil villages, for it's free from busy main roads and their associated developments. This is particularly true in the upper Ebble Valley close to Cranborne Chase and the Dorset border, where the 13-mile (21km) chalk stream rises. Here, tortuous narrow lanes link isolated farmsteads, hamlets and villages, hidden and protected in the folds of the steeply rising chalk hills.

## ALVEDISTON AND EBBESBOURNE WAKE

Norrington Manor and the nearby village of Alvediston date back to medieval times. They were associated with one of the oldest families in England, the Gawens, said to be descended from the legendary knight Sir Gawain, of King Arthur's Round Table. The original manor house was built in the time of Richard II and the Gawens completed the building after 1377. Much of the striking 14th-century stone building still stands, with some 17th-century additions. Memorials to the Gawen family, and the Wyndham family who succeeded them at Norrington after 450 years, can be seen in St Mary's Church at Alvediston, which was rebuilt in 1866 and overlooks peaceful water-meadows.

Ebbesbourne Wake nestles beside the intermittently flowing Ebble stream at the base of the downs, oblivious to 21st-century hustle and bustle. A collection of neat thatched cottages congregates around the 15th-century church, which stands on a hill, and close to the gem of a simple and unspoilt village inn – the Horseshoe.

## FOLLOWING THE HEREPATH

For hundreds, even thousands of years, this hilltop track, known as the Herepath or Salisbury Way, was one of main highways linking

Salisbury to the west, especially for pilgrims travelling to the abbeys at Wilton and Shaftesbury. In later years the route was used by horse-drawn coaches en route from London to Exeter, until improved road-making techniques in the 19th century made it possible for a new road to be built in the Nadder Valley. Its importance in the earliest days can be traced through the presence of earthworks, barrows, tumuli and, a little way east, the Iron Age settlement of Chiselbury Camp. It is now a deserted grassy track providing a fine panorama to the north across the broad, undulating and wooded Nadder Valley, and south down steep dry valleys into the narrow Ebble Valley and to lofty chalk downland beyond.

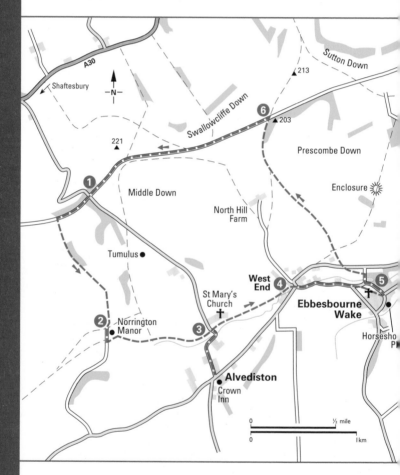

❶ Head west along the arrowed byway, the Herepath (can be flooded after heavy rain). Emerge from the copse and take the bridleway left. Descend into the Ebble Valley, keeping to the narrow enclosed path to a gate.

Continue ahead down the field-edge, following the track through two gates to Norrington Manor.

❷ Cross the track and walk between farm buildings. Where the farm track veers right, cross the stile on your left and keep to the left-hand field-edge to a stile in the corner. Cross the track and take the path ahead through the valley bottom to a gate. Keep to the left through the field to a stile and lane in Alvediston.

**3** Turn right and continue along the lane to visit the thatched Crown Inn. Retrace your steps past the stile and turn right along the drive up to St Mary's Church. When you have explored this, return down the drive and go through the field gate at the bottom. Keep to the path ahead across two fields to a gate and enter the hamlet of West End.

**4** At the road, turn right across the stream, then immediately left and follow the lane with the stream on your left. At a fork, bear left along Duck Street, then, as it begins to dip left, fork right along a footpath to the church in Ebbesbourne Wake.

**5** By the lychgate, bear left to the lane and turn right to visit the 17th-century Horseshoe pub. Otherwise, hook back left down Duck Street. At the bottom, take the footpath right, cross the bridge over the Ebble and climb the stile on your left. Follow the path diagonally right up the slope to a stile. Cross the road and the stile opposite, then bear left up the field-edge. Climb steadily, with Prescombe Down opening out on your right. Go through the metal gate on the left and continue ascending along a track to a field gate. Continue ahead, following the field-edge, crossing two stiles as you pass beside a thicket, then turn right along a byway.

**6** At a crossing of tracks at the top, turn sharp left and follow the rutted Herepath for about a mile (1.6km) back to the car parking area, with the steep escarpment of Swallowcliffe Down to your right.

**WHERE TO EAT AND DRINK** Time your walk to coincide with opening times at the Horseshoe in Ebbesbourne Wake. This unspoilt village inn offers ale from the cask, home-cooked food and a pretty flower garden. If you can't wait, then divert to the Crown Inn, a cosy free house in Alvediston with an extensive beer garden.

**WHAT TO SEE** In pride of place at the front of Alvediston churchyard is the tomb of Sir Anthony Eden (1897–1977), Earl of Avon and Conservative Prime Minister between 1955 and 1957. He lived in the brick-built 18th-century manor house close to the church.

**WHILE YOU'RE THERE** Take a leisurely drive through the delightful Ebble Valley. Begin at Berwick St John and head east through Ebbesbourne Wake to Fifield Bavant and visit St Martin's Church, one of England's smallest churches, measuring 35ft (10.6m) long and 15ft (4.6m) wide. In Broad Chalke, the largest village in the valley, you will see some fine manor houses, notably Reddish House where the photographer and designer Sir Cecil Beaton lived until his death in 1980. He is buried in the churchyard.

# Bowood Park

DISTANCE 7 miles (11.3km)    MINIMUM TIME 3hrs 30min

ASCENT/GRADIENT 360ft (110m) ▲▲▲    LEVEL OF DIFFICULTY +++

PATHS Field, woodland and parkland paths, metalled drives, pavement beside A4, former railway line

LANDSCAPE Rolling farmland and open parkland

SUGGESTED MAP AA Leisure Map 15 Swindon & Devizes

START/FINISH Grid reference: ST998710

DOG FRIENDLINESS Take particular care along busy A4 stretch

PARKING Choice of car parks in Calne

PUBLIC TOILETS Calne

Calne rose to fame producing woollen broadcloth and, up until the 18th century, the town had 20 or more mills along the River Marden. St Mary's Church owes its splendour to the generous donations of the rich clothiers and wool merchants in the 15th century. When the Industrial Revolution killed its livelihood, Calne turned to bacon-curing and the making of sausages and pies – meat processing had been a major employer in the town from the early 19th century, thanks to its location. Calne was a resting place on the main droving route from the West Country to Smithfield Market. Cattle, sheep and, more importantly pigs, which had been transported from Ireland via Bristol, passed through the town. Harris, the family butchers, took their pick from the grunting mass, eventually establishing their factory here, and in 1864 patented their bacon-curing process. Calne became the home of Wiltshire bacon and further prospered with the arrival of the railway. Now both the railway and Harris have gone, leaving this busy crossroads town with a faded air, although an ambitious plan for reconstructing the town centre is taking shape. Around the Green are the finest of Calne's Georgian houses, especially Adam House and Bentley House, classic reminders that Calne was once a prosperous market town.

## BOWOOD HOUSE

Leave the town and the busy A4 and head west to the tranquil parkland that surrounds Bowood House, the true focus of your walk. Scenic footpaths take you through the 1,000 acres (405ha) of beautiful parkland, skirting the lake, pleasure gardens and the handsome Georgian house. Originally built in 1624, the house was unfinished when it was bought by the first Earl of Shelburne in 1764. He employed some of the greatest British architects of the day, notably Robert Adam, to design the Diocletion Wing containing the library, galleries, conservatories, a laboratory and a chapel, while 'Capability' Brown laid out the gardens, which are regarded as his best surviving and most satisfactory creations.

In 1955 the original portion of this once magnificent palace had to be demolished, the Lansdownes sacrificing 200 rooms to create a habitable home and preserve the rest of their inheritance. What is left is still impressive, housing a remarkable collection of family heirlooms and works of art. The chief glory of Bowood, however, lies in its pleasure gardens, carpeted with daffodils, narcissi and bluebells in spring. Lawns roll gently down to a long tranquil lake, and there are cascades, caves and grottoes, while terraces, roses, clipped hedges and sculptures are a perfect complement to the house. If you are walking this way between mid-May and mid-June, make sure you explore the spectacular rhododendron walks.

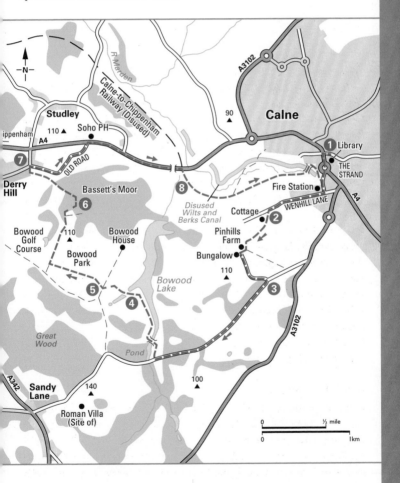

❶ Locate the library on The Strand (A4) and walk south along New Road to the roundabout. Turn right along Station Road and take the metalled footpath left opposite the fire station. Turn right on reaching Wenhill Lane and follow it out of the built-up area.

**2** On nearing a cottage, follow the waymarker left and walk along the field-edge. Just beyond the cottage, climb the bank and keep left along the field-edge to a plank bridge and stile. Keep to the left-hand field-edge and soon bear left to a stile. Follow the path right, through rough grass around Pinhills Farm to emerge opposite a bungalow and turn left along the drive.

**3** At a junction, turn sharp right along a further metalled drive and continue for a mile (1.6km). Near a bridge, take the footpath right, through a kissing gate and walk through parkland beside a pond. Cross a bridge, go through a gate and turn right alongside Bowood Lake.

**4** With Bowood House ahead of you, bear left to a gate and cross the causeway between lakes to a gate. Keep straight on up the track, following it left and then right to cross the driveway to Bowood House.

**5** Beyond a gate, keep ahead along the field-edge, soon to follow the path left straight across Bowood Park. Keep left of trees and the field boundary to a gate. Turn right along the metalled drive beside Bowood Golf Course. Where the drive turns sharp right to a cottage, keep straight on into woodland.

**6** Swing immediately right, then follow the path left, downhill through a clearing (can be boggy) along the line of telegraph poles. Turn left at the bottom of the hill and follow the woodland path uphill beside the golf course. Turn right through a break in the trees and go through the main gates to Bowood House into Derry Hill.

**7** Turn immediately right along Old Road. At the A4, turn right along the pavement. Shortly, cross to the opposite pavement and continue downhill. Pass beneath a footbridge, cross back with care and take the metalled drive immediately right.

**8** Join the former Calne-to-Chippenham railway line at Black Dog Halt. Turn left and follow this for over a mile (1.6km) back towards Calne. Cross the disused Wilts and Berks Canal and turn right along the tow path. Where the path forks keep right to reach Station Road. Retrace your steps to the town centre.

WHERE TO EAT AND DRINK There are various pubs and tea rooms in Calne, as well as the Soho pub on the A4, directly on the route of the walk. Try the Patch of Blue Café in St Mary's Courtyard in Calne for light lunches and afternoon tea. Bowood House (open daily end Mar–early Nov) has a pleasant, modern coffee shop.

WHAT TO SEE As you stroll around The Green in Calne, look for the wall plaque on Bentley House, near the church, stating that Samuel Taylor Coleridge lived and wrote here between 1814 and 1816. Note the old water pump beside the A4 in Calne, which was used to lay the dust when New Road was built in 1801. Black Dog Halt is one of many names in Wiltshire associated with Black Dog folklore.

WHILE YOU'RE THERE Off the A4 just south of Calne you will find the Atwell-Wilson Motor Museum. It contains 100 vintage and classic cars from 1924 to 1983, including Cadillacs and a model 'T' Ford, motorbikes and unusual memorabilia.

*Left: Lake in Bowood Park (Walk 26)*

# Bremhill and Maud Heath's Causeway

| | |
|---|---|
| DISTANCE 4 miles (6.4km) | MINIMUM TIME 2hrs |

ASCENT/GRADIENT 295ft (90m) ▲▲▲     LEVEL OF DIFFICULTY ✦✦✦

PATHS Field paths, bridle paths, metalled roads, many stiles

LANDSCAPE Gently rolling farmland, downland escarpment

SUGGESTED MAP AA Leisure Map 15 Swindon & Devizes

START/FINISH Grid reference: ST980730

DOG FRIENDLINESS Keep dogs on leads at all times

PARKING Bremhill church

PUBLIC TOILETS None on route

Nestling on the upper slopes of Wick Hill, surrounded by lush pastureland, isolated farmsteads and leafy lanes, tiny Bremhill is a timeless downland village complete with an ancient church, a fine stepped medieval cross and a single street lined with pretty ragstone cottages. Surprisingly, for such a pastoral area, there is much to interest the casual rambler undertaking this short walk, in addition to the absorbing views across the north Wiltshire plain to the Cotswold hills from the mile-long (1.6km) stretch of bridle path across Wick Hill.

## WILLIAM LISLE BOWLES – RECTOR AND POET

Reverend William Lisle Bowles (1762–1850), rector of St Martin's Church in Bremhill from 1803 to 1844, lived in the vicarage, now Bremhill Court, adjacent to the church. Bowles was not only an eccentric, filling his garden with grottoes, urns and hermitages and keeping sheep in the churchyard with their bells tuned in thirds and fifths, he was also a poet. His literary friends, such as Wordsworth, Coleridge, Southey and Charles Lamb, were all part of the considerable literary circle centred upon Bowood House. Although much of his poetry was derided, it was his now forgotten sonnets, published in nine editions, that influenced the whole school of poetry and gained admiration from Coleridge and Wordsworth. Scour the churchyard and you will find some examples of Bowles' poetry, as this eccentric vicar was unable to resist breaking into verse on tombstones, monuments and even a sundial!

## MAUD HEATH

One of Bowles' less impressive verses is inscribed on the monument you will pass on top of Wick Hill. Erected by Bowles and the Marquis of Lansdowne in 1838, it commemorates Maud Heath, a local widow, who in 1474 made a bequest of land and property in Chippenham to provide an income to build and maintain a causeway from Wick Hill through the Avon marshes to Chippenham, a distance of around 4.5 miles (7.2km). Although starting from the top of a hill, much of the land along the route was low lying and prone to flooding in winter, so her aim was to provide a dry pathway for country people to walk to market.

For much of its route the Causeway is little more than a raised path, but the most interesting section can be found at Kellaways, where the way is elevated some 6ft (1.8m) on stone arches as it crosses the River Avon, a remarkable feat of engineering for its time.

On top of the monument on Wick Hill, Maud is depicted in a shawl and bonnet with her basket by her side. Although she has been described as a market woman, it seems unlikely that a lady wealthy enough to provide land and property on this scale would have been walking to market herself. You will see the beginning of the Causeway as you cross the hilltop road where a tablet states 'From this Wick Hill begins the praise of Maud Heath's gift to these highways'.

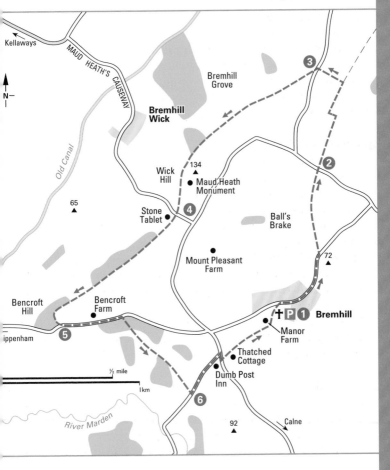

**1** With your back to the church, turn right and walk downhill through the village of Bremhill. Begin to climb and take the arrowed path left to go through a gate. Proceed straight on below the bank along the field-edge to a stile in the corner. Bear diagonally right, heading uphill over two stiles to a lane.

**2** Cross the stile opposite and cross a paddock to a further stile. Bear slightly left to a stile in the field corner and walk along the left-hand edge to a stile. In the next field look out for and pass over a stile on your left and head straight across the field to a gate and lane.

**3** Turn left, then immediately bear right to a gate. Join the waymarked bridle path along the right-hand field-edge to a gate. Maintain direction through several fields and gates to reach the monument to Maud Heath on top of Wick Hill.

**4** Continue to cross a lane via gates, passing the stone tablet and inscription identifying the beginning of Maud Heath's Causeway. Follow the bridle path along the crest of the hill through seven fields via gates and bear left before woodland to reach a gate and lane at the top of Bencroft Hill.

**5** Turn left, pass Bencroft Farm and a bungalow, continue on the lane, then take the waymarked path right, through woodland, bearing left on nearing a gate to cross a stile. Proceed straight across the field on a defined path, cross a stile and remain on the path, keeping over to the right of the pasture to a stile to the left of a bungalow.

**6** Turn left along the lane, heading uphill to a junction beside the Dumb Post Inn. Turn right, then left along the drive to a thatched cottage. Go through a squeeze stile and keep to the left-hand edge of the field through a gate and stile to reach a stile in the field corner. Walk in front of Manor Farm to reach a gate leading into Bremhill churchyard. Bear right along the path back to your car.

WHERE TO EAT AND DRINK The Dumb Post Inn, an 18th-century stone and tile building, provides welcome refreshment towards the end of the walk. Relax in the garden on summer days and enjoy the views towards Bowood Park.

WHAT TO SEE On the outside of the north wall of St Martin's Church in Bremhill you will find a carved stone memorial to 'a poor old soldier', Benjamin Tremblin, who died in 1822 at the age of 92. The verse, written by the Reverend Bowles, commemorates the notable actions and commanders he had witnessed.

WHILE YOU'RE THERE Follow the route of Maud Heath's Causeway to Kellaways to view the path where it crosses 60 raised arches and see the sundial monument, erected in 1698 and inscribed with the story of Maud Heath's legacy.

# Heytesbury Chalk Stream

DISTANCE 4 miles (6.4km)   MINIMUM TIME 2hrs

ASCENT/GRADIENT 49ft (15m) ▲▲▲   LEVEL OF DIFFICULTY ✦✦✦

PATHS Field paths and bridleways, several stiles

LANDSCAPE River valley and lofty chalk downland

SUGGESTED MAP OS Explorer 143 Warminster & Trowbridge

START/FINISH Grid reference: ST926425

DOG FRIENDLINESS Lead required around livestock and village lanes

PARKING Plenty of room along wide village street

PUBLIC TOILETS None on route

The River Wylye threads its way through some of the finest downland scenery in the county on its journey from Warminster to Salisbury. Iron Age hill-forts, ancient tumuli and barrows litter the chalk downland, much of it now extensively farmed. In the valley, away from the A36, are pretty picture-postcard villages, including the charmingly named Knook, Boyton, Sherrington and Corton.

## HISTORIC HEYTESBURY

Heytesbury is an ancient borough and it's worth allowing time to explore before or after your walk. Wealth and prosperity came to the village through the prominence of one family in the 14th century – the Hungerfords – who acquired land and purchased manors across the southwest, including a complex of manors in the upper Wylye Valley. Sir Walter Hungerford fought at Agincourt in 1415 and became Treasurer of England in 1428. He also founded and endowed a chapel in Salisbury Cathedral and founded the Almshouses, or Hospital of St John, that stand opposite the Angel Inn in the village. Under the Hungerfords, the Wylye estates became noted for sheep farming and Heytesbury became the main wool warehouse of the family.

Cloth production began in Heytesbury in the mid-15th century but it wasn't until the 18th century that the proximity of the River Wylye attracted cloth mills along its course. Plans to develop the industry never materialised and when its borough status was lost in the Great Reform Act of 1832, Heytesbury gradually declined.

Sadly, the village lacks buildings of any special interest due to the 'Great Fire' of 1765. Notable exceptions include Heytesbury Mill, Parsonage Farm to the south of the church, 69 High Street and Heytesbury House, which stands across the A36 bypass on the site of the medieval mansion of East Court, once the residence of the Hungerford family. In 1926 Heytesbury House became the home of the respected World War I poet and writer Siegfried Sassoon.

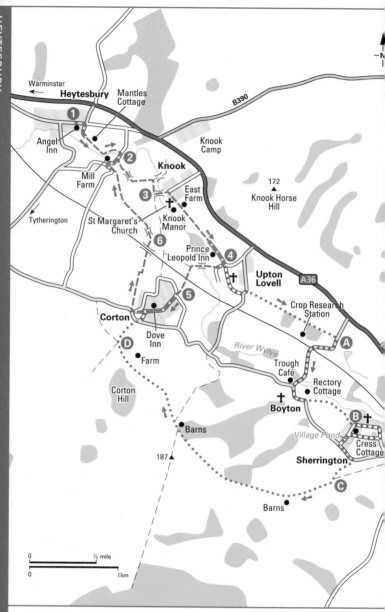

**1** Head east along the village street, pass the Angel Inn and turn right down Mantles Lane. Where it curves right to become Mill Street, take the footpath left along a drive beside the River Wylye. Bear right on to the footpath in front of Mantles Cottage, go through a kissing gate and walk

along the right-hand edge of pasture, soon to bear slightly left on nearing Mill Farm to reach a gate.

**2** Beyond a further gate, turn right across the bridge, then follow the marked track immediately left and soon cross a footbridge. Keep left at a junction of ways then, just before a further footbridge, turn left through a metal gate and bear right along the field-edge. Go through the gap in the corner and bear half left across the field towards thatched cottages to the riverbank and bear right to a redundant stile and junction of paths.

**3** Turn left across the footbridge, pass Knook Manor and St Margaret's Church, then turn right by the post-box and soon pass East Farm on a track (which can be very messy after rain). Keep right, and at two gates, go past the left-hand gate and proceed ahead along the fenced grassy track to another gate. Continue on the metalled lane into Upton Lovell.

**4** At a crossroads, take the signed footpath right, then just before the drive to Hatch House, follow the path left to a footbridge over the river. Go through a gate and proceed ahead along the field-edge to a metal gate. Turn left through the kissing gate, walk along the hedged path

and cross the railway with great care via gates and steps. Continue to a lane in Corton.

**5** Turn left and then bear right through the village, eventually passing the Dove Inn. At the T-junction, take the arrowed path through the kissing gate on your right. Head across the field on a defined path to a kissing gate and keep ahead through a gate to a further kissing gate. Go along the right-hand edge of the field and shortly go through a kissing gate, turn left along the field-edge to a kissing gate and pass beneath the railway.

**6** Cross a footbridge, go through a kissing gate and walk beside the right-hand hedge to a gate. From here, follow the grassy track ahead. Cross another stile and keep to the track until you reach a lane. Turn right and follow it through the complex of buildings at Mill Farm and across the river to rejoin your outward route beside the River Wylye back into Heytesbury.

**WHERE TO EAT AND DRINK** Both the Angel Inn in Heytesbury and the Dove Inn at Corton offer excellent food and real ale, while the Prince Leopold Inn at Upton Lovell also boasts a riverside garden. On the longer route, try the Trough Café at The Ginger Piggery farm centre at Boyton for home-cooked dishes and cakes (open Wed–Sat).

**WHAT TO SEE** In Knook, note the interesting stone tympanum of 1623 above the south door of St Margaret's Church. The intricate carved motifs are early 11th century. Boyton church is the resting place of the chivalrous crusader Sir Alexander Gifford, whose striking effigy shows him crosslegged with an otter at his feet. Also in Boyton, look out for the old signs with a religious theme on the exterior of the church and Rectory Cottage.

**WHILE YOU'RE THERE** Seek out the hamlet of Tytherington across the valley from Heytesbury to view the single-cell chapel that dates from 1083 and was endowed by Empress Matilda, mother of Henry II, in 1140. At Codford St Mary you will find the second largest Anzac War Grave Cemetery in Britain, with the graves of nearly 100 New Zealand and Australian troops who died on the battlefields during World War I.

# Wylye Valley Villages

DISTANCE 8.5 miles (13.7km)    MINIMUM TIME 4hrs

ASCENT/GRADIENT 360ft (110m) ▲▲▲    LEVEL OF DIFFICULTY ✦✦✦

SEE MAP AND INFORMATION PANEL FOR WALK 28

At the crossroads, Point ❹, keep straight on to the church and then follow the path ahead to a drive. Turn left, then left again at the lane, soon to bear off right at the bend on to a bridleway. Enter a field and keep right along the edge to the corner. Keep ahead along a straight path through a tunnel of trees to a field. Proceed straight across towards a bungalow, crossing two stiles to a lane, Point Ⓐ. Turn right and continue across the railway and the River Wylye into Boyton.

Don't miss St Mary's Church in Boyton, approached along an elegant driveway that also leads to the handsome 17th-century manor house. Inside, the Gifford Chapel has a great wheel window. Pevsner described it as a 'tour-de-force'.

At the junction, turn right for the Trough Café, or to visit Boyton church. Otherwise turn left, pass Rectory Cottage then, at a right-hand bend, go through the metal kissing gate ahead and bear left across a field to a gate. Follow the path ahead, to the right of the hedge, to a gap on your left. Turn right on a drive, then bear left into Sherrington, Point Ⓑ.

Unusually dedicated to two Middle Eastern saints, Cosmas and Damian, the little church possesses some 14th-century glass and an almost complete set of wall-texts used for religious education purposes during the Elizabethan and Jacobean periods.

Past the church, follow the road as it bends up right, and take the first road on the right. Pass the bottom of the village pond, and turn left at Cress Cottage. Walk up through the village, and turn left at the T-junction. In 150yds (137m), cross the stile on the right and walk up the left-hand field-edge to a stile. Turn right and soon bear diagonally left uphill to stile. Continue straight over the field to a further stile and turn right along the track, Point Ⓒ.

Look back across the valley to view the Rising Sun Badge etched into Lamb Down. At 175ft (53m) by 150ft (46m) tall it is a version of the badge used by Anzac troops and was cut out by Australians stationed at Codford in 1916.

Gradually ascend, keep right on merging with a farm road and pass the barns on the left. Continue for 1.75 miles (2.8km) to reach a major crossing of routes, Point Ⓓ. Turn right, then almost immediately bear left down a bridle path into Corton. Cross a lane and descend to the road by the thatched cob wall of the Dove Inn. Turn left and join Walk 28 just after Point ❺.

# Around Devizes

DISTANCE 4.25 miles (6.8km)　MINIMUM TIME 2hrs

ASCENT/GRADIENT 180ft (55m) ▲▲▲　LEVEL OF DIFFICULTY ✦✦✦

PATHS Pavements, canal tow path

LANDSCAPE Town streets and canal

SUGGESTED MAP OS Explorers 156 Chippenham & Bradford-on-Avon;
157 Marlborough & Savernake Forest

START/FINISH Grid reference: SU004617 (on Explorer 157)

DOG FRIENDLINESS Dogs can be off lead along tow path

PARKING Devizes Wharf car park

PUBLIC TOILETS Car park off Snuff Street, Devizes

Devizes is Wiltshire's principal market town. It grew up around the
castle, built by Bishop Osmund of Salisbury in 1080. It burnt down and
was rebuilt in 1138 by Bishop Roger of Salisbury, builder of Old Sarum
and Malmesbury Castle. The castle was demolished by Cromwell's forces
shortly after the Battle of Devizes in 1645 and the present-day building
is a Victorian folly. Devizes, noted for its two fine Norman churches,
has held a market since receiving its first Charter in 1141. Following
the demise of the castle, the large marketplace became the focal point
and the town prospered on the wool trade and dairy produce from the
Vale of Pewsey.

## MONDAY MARKET STREET

In the early 19th century, Devizes held the largest corn market in the
west of England. The wool trade's prosperity is mirrored in the wool
merchants' 18th-century town houses in St John's and Long Street, and
around the marketplace. Other notable buildings are the Elizabethan
timber-framed houses in St John's Alley, Great Porch House in Monday
Market Street and the 16th-century Bear Hotel.

## WADWORTH'S AND A HINT OF HOPS

The town's marketplace is known for its splendid 19th-century cross.
One inscription reads: 'Erected by Henry, Viscount Sidmouth, as a
memorial of his grateful attachment to the borough of Devizes, of
which he has been recorder thirty years and of which he was six times
unanimously chosen a representative in parliament. Anno Domini
1814.' The other inscription recalls Ruth Pierce, who asked Heaven to
strike her dead if she lied during a disagreement over money at the local
market. According to the inscription: 'she fell instantly and expired.'
Wadworth's Brewery, a red-brick Victorian building, dominates the

northern end of Market Place. To learn more about the town's history, visit the local library in Sheep Street.

## CAEN HILL – THE GIANT'S VERTEBRAE

Not far out of town is one of the area's most fascinating landmarks – Caen Hill Locks. This famous flight, nicknamed the 'giant's vertebrae',

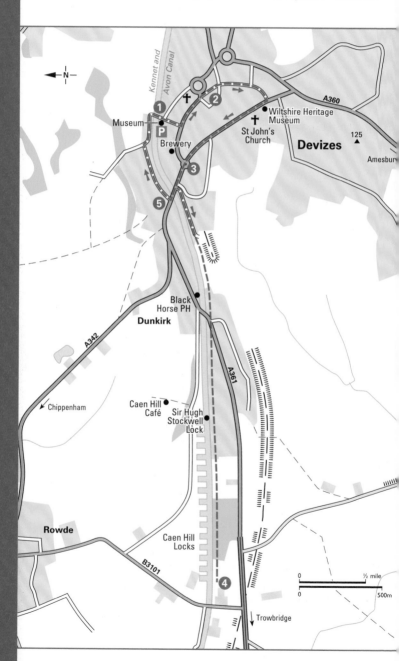

is one of the great wonders of the canal era. Completed in 1810, to carry the Kennet and Avon Canal to a height of 237ft (72m), it consists of 29 locks in all, extending over 2 miles (3.2km). The canalside at Devizes Wharf has also been revitalized in recent years. The former timbered and balconied granary, built in 1810, is now the headquarters of the Kennet and Avon Canal Trust and houses a small canal museum. The warehouse, occupied by the Wharf Theatre, was equipped with a huge crane that could unload goods straight into the building from the boats.

❶ From the car park, walk back down Wharf Street and turn left along New Park Street, passing 18th-century Brownston House and St Mary's Church. At the roundabout, cross the road and walk down Monday Market Street, passing the White Bear.

❷ Follow Maryport Street and, on reaching a crossroads, keep ahead along Sheep Street, passing the town's library, and then Bridewell Street to reach Long Street. Turn right, pass the Wiltshire Heritage Museum, historic St John's Church and the Town Hall to enter the Market Place.

❸ Continue along Northgate Street, keeping ahead at the roundabout by Wadworth's Brewery. At the canal bridge, take the path right, signed 'Caen Hill Locks via subway', and join the tow path. Pass under the road and head west to reach the A361. Pass under it and follow the tow path to Caen Hill Locks.

❹ At the bottom of the flight, turn round and retrace your steps back uphill, possibly pausing at the cafe across the bridge by the Sir Hugh Stockwell Lock. Recross the A361 and walk back to the subway.

❺ Leave the tow path to cross the road bridge and join the northern bank of the canal. Follow the tow path to the next bridge, cross it and turn right to pass the Kennet and Avon Canal Museum at Devizes Wharf. The car park, where the walk began, is immediately adjacent.

**WHERE TO EAT AND DRINK** Most pubs in Devizes serve Wadworth's ales. Try the friendly Bear Hotel in the Market Place, the Castle Hotel in New Park Street or the Black Horse just off the route of the walk on the A361. The Bistro (just off the Market Place) is good for coffee and light lunches. The Caen Hill Café, at the top of the flight, is open daily and there is also a cafe in the town's Wharf. Alternatively, try one of the nearby village pubs – perhaps the George and Dragon at Rowde.

**WHAT TO SEE** As you stroll through the streets, watch for the regular delivery of the local brew, Wadworth's, by a brewer's dray, pulled by a magnificent pair of Shire horses. The town's marketplace might be familiar to film buffs. Scenes from the 1967 film *Far From the Madding Crowd* were shot here.

**WHILE YOU'RE THERE** Visit the excellent Wiltshire Heritage Museum in Long Street, which boasts one of the finest prehistoric collections in Europe, tracing the history of Wiltshire and its people from the earliest times to the present day.

*Overleaf: The flight of locks near Devizes (Walk 30)*

# East Knoyle

**DISTANCE** 5 miles (8km)     **MINIMUM TIME** 2hrs 30min

**ASCENT/GRADIENT** 590ft (180m) ▲▲▲     **LEVEL OF DIFFICULTY** +++

**PATHS** Field paths, woodland bridle paths, metalled lanes

**LANDSCAPE** Wooded hillside, undulating farmland, village streets

**SUGGESTED MAP** OS Explorer 143 Warminster & Trowbridge

**START/FINISH** Grid reference: ST879305

**DOG FRIENDLINESS** Lead required for short stretches of road walking

**PARKING** East Knoyle village hall, adjacent to church

**PUBLIC TOILETS** None on route

Sleepy East Knoyle clings to the slopes of a greensand ridge on the northern flanks of the Nadder Valley. Comprising four distinct hamlets – Underhill, Milton, Upton and The Green – it is an appealing scattered parish characterised by charming stone-built cottages and a myriad tiny lanes that meet close to Windmill Hill, which at 650ft (198m) offers unrivalled views across the Blackmore Vale into Dorset. This walk explores some of the peaceful paths that link the hamlets. It loops round to West Knoyle in the Sem Valley before ascending Windmill Hill.

## THE WREN CONNECTION

The heart of the village is Underhill, where you will find the post office stores, the ancient Church of St Mary the Virgin and several reminders that East Knoyle was the birthplace of Sir Christopher Wren. His father was appointed rector of East Knoyle in 1623 and married the daughter of a local squire. The rectory in which they lived now forms part of Knoyle Place, an elegant Georgian house built in 1799. Christopher was born in 1632 in a cottage at the bottom of Wise Lane, opposite the present village shop, Wren's Shop. The cottage was demolished in 1878. Wren's interests lay in mathematics and architecture and his greatest opportunity in the latter came with the rebuilding that followed the London fire of 1666. He re-planned the city and supervised the rebuilding of 51 churches, his most famous design being that of St Paul's Cathedral.

## KNOYLE CHURCH AND RECTOR WREN

The most visible reminder of the Wren family can be seen in the church. Pevsner said that every Wiltshire tourist should make a point of seeing this late 13th-century church, notably the chancel. What really makes it interesting are the intricate plaster wall decorations. Designed by Wren's father in 1639, they are unique in an English parish church. The decorations brought Dr Wren, an ardent Royalist, trouble during the Civil War. It is said that Roundheads interrupted him working on the plasterwork and thinking he was occupied on idolatrous Papist works of art, they removed him by force and damaged many of the decorations. Although later allowed to continue, he was brought to trial in 1647 accused of 'heretical practices', but doubtless his real crime was that of being a Royalist. Although the charge of heresy was not sustained, he was fined £40 and his living sequestrated.

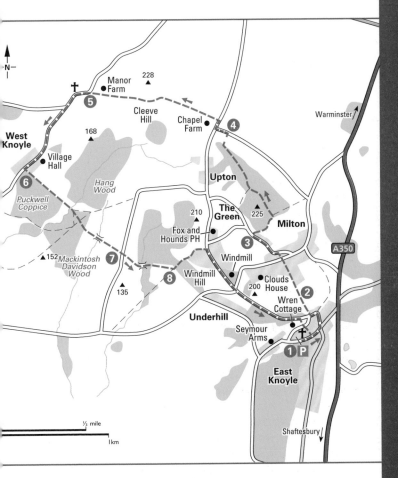

❶ Turn left out of the car park into the village. Turn left up Wise Lane. Bear left and take the bridleway signed to the right after No. 118. Keep ahead along the grass track where the drive veers left.

❷ Keep ahead uphill, soon to bear left along a metalled drive. On reaching the stable buildings of Clouds House, take the unmarked path to the right, downhill, passing Park Cottage to reach the lane in Milton. Cross over and bear left along the lower lane.

❸ Pass Manor Farm and a thatched cottage on your right, then climb the bank, turn right behind a cottage to a gate and climb through the edge of woodland. At the top, bear half left along the woodland path and descend to soon reach an unmarked bridle path. Hook left, then right at the next junction and follow the woodland path downhill to a lane.

4 Turn left, then right at the T-junction. Take the bridle path left beyond Chapel Farm, immediately forking right along a track to a gate. Continue ahead along the field-edge, following it over the top and left to a gate in the field corner. Follow the bridle path and gradually descend off Cleeve Hill, passing through two gates and Manor Farm to the lane in West Knoyle.

5 Keep ahead and continue through the village for 0.5 miles (800m). Pass the village hall and continue to 'Woodside'.

6 Just beyond turn left through a Woodland Trust gateway towards Mackintosh Davidson Wood. Keep ahead through a wooden farm gate, just outside the woodland edge on your right. Continue through two more gates, cross a small valley, and keep ahead through a gap in the hedge to a footbridge with a gate on each side. Bear slightly left past a small woodland spur to a stile in the far hedge.

7 Turn right along the track, then left over two stiles and bear diagonally right, soon to descend steeply to a stile and copse. Cross a footbridge and a second stile and keep straight ahead, uphill through the trees to enter a field. Continue beside woodland to a stile in the top left-hand corner.

8 Follow the bridleway uphill through woodland. At a junction, turn left, then at the top, bear right into a cul-de-sac to reach the lane. Turn left for the Fox and Hounds. Turn right to reach Windmill Hill, keep ahead at a crossroads and descend into East Knoyle. Take the metalled footpath beside Wren Cottage, cross a lane and descend steps into the churchyard. At the road, turn right to get back to the car park.

**WHERE TO EAT AND DRINK** The creeper-covered Seymour Arms on the edge of East Knoyle offers generous home-cooked food and Wadworth's ales. A short diversion at Windmill Hill will bring you to the Fox and Hounds at The Green for hearty pub meals, a good range of beers and great views from the garden.

**WHAT TO SEE** Note the elegant and appropriately named hilltop mansion, Clouds, as you ascend towards Milton. It was built for the Wyndham family by Philip Webb in 1886 at a cost of £80,000, but had to be rebuilt in 1891 at a further cost of £35,000 following a fire.

**WHILE YOU'RE THERE** Nine miles (14.5km) west along the A303 is Stourhead, one of the National Trust's finest gardens. Designed by Henry Hoare II and laid out between 1741 and 1780, it is an outstanding example of an English landscaped garden, with classical temples set around a lake and magnificent woodland with exotic trees. Enjoy views of the Palladian mansion on the estate walks (see walks 43 and 44).

# Around Fonthill

| | |
|---|---|
| DISTANCE 4.25 miles (6.8km) | MINIMUM TIME 2hrs |

ASCENT/GRADIENT 278ft (85m) ▲▲▲     LEVEL OF DIFFICULTY ✚✚✚

PATHS Tracks, field and woodland paths, parkland, some road walking

LANDSCAPE Wooded hillside, rolling parkland

SUGGESTED MAP OS Explorer 143 Warminster & Trowbridge

START/FINISH Grid reference: ST933316

DOG FRIENDLINESS Dogs required to be under strict control around lake

PARKING Lay-by close to southern end of Fonthill Lake

PUBLIC TOILETS None on route

The vast Fonthill Estate lies tucked away on the rolling northern flanks of the unspoilt Nadder Valley between Tisbury, one of Wiltshire's oldest small towns, and the charming village of Hindon. This wonderful short walk explores Fonthill Park, with its beautiful tree-fringed lake and splendid triumphal-style gateway, attributed to Inigo Jones, and ridge-top woodland and pastures between the estate villages of Fonthill Bishop and Fonthill Gifford. Fonthill House lies secluded on a wooded hillside above the sweeping parkland and to the casual passer-by it is the epitome of a perfect country estate. It is also the setting for the most fantastic story to be found in Wiltshire.

## FONTHILL'S ECCENTRIC OWNER

Fonthill Estate was acquired by William Beckford, a Lord Mayor of London in the mid-18th century. Having built the Palladian mansion, Fonthill Splendens, he died in 1770 leaving a large fortune from sugar plantations to his 10-year-old son William. An utterly spoilt, capricious and extravagant child, England's richest young man embraced Romanticism in all its forms, travelling across Europe and writing weird and fantastic tales, notably *Vathek*, a seminal Gothic novel about a hero who lived alone in a mighty tower. Unlike other Romantic writers, the eccentric Beckford had the means to indulge his fantasies.

## BECKFORD'S GREAT GOTHIC FOLLY

Beckford surrounded his estate with a wall 12 miles (19.3km) long and 12ft (3.6m) high, and in 1796 commissioned James Wyatt to build his Gothic dream palace, a grandiose, partly ruined 'abbey', deep in woodland to the west of Fonthill Lake. Beckford and the slapdash Wyatt built in a great hurry, employing 500 men to work day and night, and kept fires burning to prevent plaster and cement from freezing. By 1800, the cruciform building had a central tower 275ft (84m) high and, although unfinished, work had progressed enough for

Beckford to entertain Nelson and Lady Hamilton here. Although never completed, the scale of the plan for the abbey was such that the tower was intended to have a spire, elevating it to 450ft (137m), overtopping Salisbury Cathedral by 50ft (15m). Beckford finally moved into the abbey in 1807.

For the next 15 years he lived in the unfinished building as a recluse, then, in 1823, when his funds had virtually run dry, he sold the estate to John Farquhar, an equally eccentric gunpowder millionaire, and moved to Bath. Two years later, owing to Wyatt's negligence and dishonest builders, the massive foundationless tower collapsed in a storm, bringing down much of the rest of the abbey. Beckford, meanwhile, was busy building an Italianate tower on the top of Lansdown Hill. Fortunately this didn't collapse and is now the finest surviving example of his work. Fonthill was the classic folly, 'the most prodigious romantic folly in England' as Pevsner described it. Sadly, you are unable to see the abbey remains, a small turret room and the battlemented cloisters, as they are incorporated into a house at the end of a private drive.

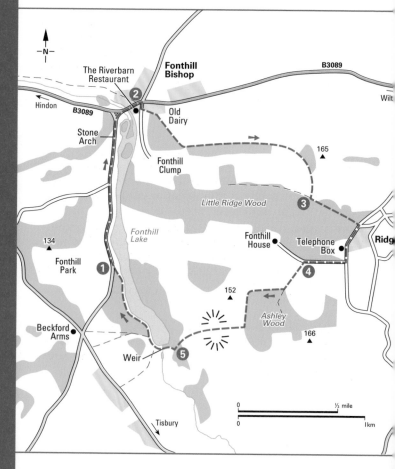

**1** With your back to the lay-by, turn right along the road (this can be busy) that traverses Fonthill Park beside the lake for just over 0.5 miles (800m). Pass beneath the magnificent stone arch and shortly bear right to the B3089. Keep to the right along the pavement into the pretty village of Fonthill Bishop.

**2** Turn right just beyond the bus shelter on to a metalled track. After a few paces, turn left on to a waymarked bridleway through the Old Dairy. Keep left and join the track that winds uphill towards woodland. Follow the grassy track beside Fonthill Clump and keep to the main track above the valley. In 0.5 miles (800m) fork right downhill into Little Ridge Wood.

**3** Begin to ascend and at a T-junction turn left and keep left at the next two junctions, following the wide path to a gate and lane. Turn right through the hamlet of Ridge.

Pass the telephone box, walk uphill and bear off right, following the signposted footpath along the drive to Fonthill House.

**4** In 0.25 miles (400m), fork left with the footpath sign to follow a track between paddocks and through a gateway. In 200yds (183m), fork right with a yellow arrow and walk beside woodland. On entering an open field, turn left along the field-edge, turning right at the corner and keeping the hedge on your left to gradually descend towards woodland.

**5** Walk down through the woods (steep in parts). Bear left, then right along a gravel track beside Fonthill Lake. Cross the weir to a gate. Disregard the track which goes ahead uphill and instead bear off to the right along the lakeside edge. Follow the well-established path through a gate, eventually returning to the parking area.

**WHERE TO EAT AND DRINK**  With its welcoming atmosphere and pretty riverside garden, The Riverbarn Restaurant in Fonthill Bishop offers an appealing range of sandwiches and light lunches, as well as afternoon tea (closed Wed). Alternatively, try the excellent Beckford Arms, 0.5 miles (800m) south from the lay-by.

**WHAT TO SEE**  Only a wing (a pair of cottages) of Fonthill Splendens remains beside the present Fonthill House. The rest was pulled down by Beckford before he decided to build his Gothic fantasy elsewhere on the estate. Take a closer look at Fonthill Lake. It was used as a location for the filming of Joanne Harris' novel *Chocolat*, when a mock galleon was deliberately blown up here.

**WHILE YOU'RE THERE**  Enjoy a stroll around Hindon, 2 miles (3.2km) north. Founded by the Bishops of Winchester between 1220 and 1250 and handsomely rebuilt by Wyatt following a fire in 1754, it has a wide attractive High Street lined with stone cottages and two fine inns. Visit Tisbury to see the largest medieval tithe barn in England, situated amid a fine collection of 14th- and 15th-century buildings at Place Farm.

# Tollard Royal

DISTANCE 4.5 miles (7.2km)    MINIMUM TIME 2hrs 30min

ASCENT/GRADIENT 616ft (188m) ▲▲▲    LEVEL OF DIFFICULTY ✦✦✦

PATHS Field and woodland paths, bridle paths and tracks

LANDSCAPE Chalk downland, sheltered combes, woodland

SUGGESTED MAP OS Explorer 118 Shaftesbury & Cranborne Chase

START/FINISH Grid reference: ST944178

DOG FRIENDLINESS Lead required through Ashcombe Bottom

PARKING Limited spaces by pond in Tollard Royal

PUBLIC TOILETS None on route

This tranquil corner of south Wiltshire lies in the heart of Cranborne Chase, with its breezy ridges and secluded dry valleys or 'bottoms' – one of which hides the village of Tollard Royal. This walk leads you around the Rushmore Estate and offers the option to ascend Win Green Hill, one of the highest points in Wiltshire at 911ft (278m).

## A ROYAL FOREST

Tangled copses and a belt of woodland are all that remain of the great forest that covered an area of some 90 square miles (233sq km). The oldest part is centred around Tollard Royal. King John hunted on the Chase and owned a small estate at Tollard, hence the 'Royal' in the village name. His lodge was on the site which is now occupied by King John's House, an elegant Elizabethan manor house near the church. By the 18th century, the forest had become a refuge for poachers, smugglers and vagabonds. After hunting rights ended in 1828, Lord Rivers destroyed much of the ancient forest, reducing it to more manageable proportions.

## THE 'FATHER OF ENGLISH ARCHAEOLOGY'

General Augustus Pitt-Rivers (1827–1900) inherited the Rushmore Estate in 1880. He found fame as a scientist and archaeologist and devoted the last 20 years of his life to excavating archaeological sites on the estate, resulting in five volumes of notes and sketches. He built a private museum in Farnham, 3 miles (4.8km) away, to house his models and local collections. The museum was open every day, free of charge, and visited by thousands of people a year. It closed in the 1960s and most of the exhibits went to Oxford University, although you can see scale models, drawings and artefacts in the Salisbury and South Wiltshire Museum in Salisbury. Pitt-Rivers died at Rushmore in 1900 and you will find a memorial to the family in St Peter ad Vincula Church in Tollard Royal.

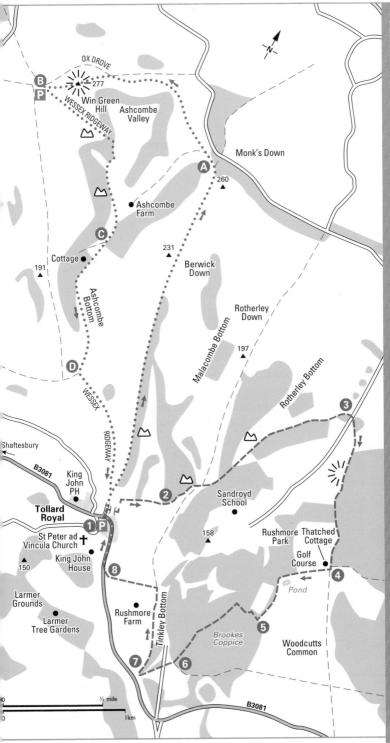

OX DROVE

B
P

WESSEX RIDGEWAY

Win Green
Hill

277

Ashcombe
Valley

Monk's Down

A

260

Ashcombe
Farm

C

Berwick
Down

231

Cottage

191

Ashcombe
Bottom

Rotherley
Down

Malacombe Bottom

197

D

WESSEX

Rotherley Bottom

RIDGEWAY

3

Shaftesbury

B3081

King
John
PH

2

Tollard
Royal

1 P

St Peter ad
Vincula Church

Sandroyd
School

150

King John
House

8

158

Rushmore
Park

Thatched
Cottage

Golf
Course

4

Larmer
Grounds

Larmer
Tree Gardens

Rushmore
Farm

Tinkley Bottom

Brookes
Coppice

Pond

5

Woodcutts
Common

7

6

½ mile

1km

B3081

**1** Facing the pond, turn left along the metalled track and take the waymarked path right across the footbridge to a stile. Follow the narrow path half left uphill through scrub. Go through a gate at the top corner and along the left-hand field-edge. Keep ahead, pass a copse, and bear left through gates into the adjacent field. Keep to the right-hand edge, following a line of electricity poles downhill to a gate and stile.

**2** Bear diagonally left and steeply descend to a gate and junction of paths in the valley bottom. Take the track right, through a gate and continue to a fork of tracks. Steeply ascend the grassy track ahead and follow it beside woodland for 0.5 miles (800m). Bear right through trees to a metalled lane.

**3** Turn right, then left before the gates to Rushmore Park. Keep to the established track, with cameo views across the park, heading gently downhill to a crossing of paths by the golf course.

**4** Turn right, pass in front of a cottage and keep to the path alongside the fairway (do not follow the track right) until you reach redundant stone gate posts. Pass beside the gate posts and keep ahead, soon passing a pond and bearing left beside the woods on your right.

**5** Bear right through a gate into the woodland and follow the yellow waymarker sharp right through the trees. At first ill-defined, the path soon bears left to become a clear route (yellow arrows) through Brookes Coppice, to reach a T-junction with a track.

**6** Turn left, cross the drive and stile diagonally opposite to the right, and bear slightly left downhill to a gate in the field corner. In a few paces, take the second arrowed path sharp right.

**7** Follow the track through Tinkley Bottom to a gate and pass below Rushmore Farm. On passing through the second of two gateways, turn immediately left and walk uphill to a pair of gates. Go through the left-hand gate and follow the wire fence on your right through two paddocks to reach a small steel gate.

**8** Take the path ahead and bear diagonally right downhill to a gate and the B3081. Keep ahead into Tollard Royal back to the pond and your car.

WHERE TO EAT AND DRINK  Seek rest and refreshment at the King John pub in Tollard Royal before tackling the energetic longer loop, Walk 34.

WHAT TO SEE  In the nave of St Peter ad Vincula Church (St Peter in Chains) in Tollard Royal you will see a 14th-century cross-legged effigy of Sir William Payne, who died in 1388. The armour is of banded mail, a rare example found on only four other effigies in England.

WHILE YOU'RE THERE  Visit Larmer Tree Gardens just off the A354 south of Tollard Royal. Created in 1880 by General Pitt-Rivers, they contain a collection of Colonial and Oriental buildings, a Roman temple and an open-air theatre. Teas available on Sundays only.

# To Win Green Hill

DISTANCE 5.25 miles (8.4km)    MINIMUM TIME 2hrs 30min

ASCENT/GRADIENT 541ft (165m) ▲▲▲    LEVEL OF DIFFICULTY ✚✚✚

SEE MAP AND INFORMATION PANEL FOR WALK 33

Walk along the metalled track, disregard the path taken on Walk 33, then bear right at a fork along the signed 'Byway to Win Green' and steeply ascend the stony track. Remain on this established track as it steadily climbs to the top of Berwick Down. Continue to climb, the track curving left to reach a junction of ways at the summit of Monk's Down, Point Ⓐ. Ignore the metalled track on your right and proceed ahead, keeping right at the fork to follow the ancient Ox Drove track along the top of the chalk downland.

Stay on this lofty track around the top of the Ashcombe Valley, and soon reach the cattle grid and National Trust sign at Win Green Hill. Fork left here through a gate and ascend the grassy path to the clump of beech trees at the summit. Pass the trig point and a topographic table. Keep ahead to the car park at Point Ⓑ, and turn left to join the grassy path close to the right-hand fence.

Owned by the National Trust, Win Green Hill is characterised by a steep scarp face and long sweeping slopes, the chalk supporting a rich variety of plant species, including the burnt orchid, round-headed campion and yellow-wort.

Shortly, cross a stile on your right to join the Wessex Ridgeway. Disregard the swing gate on the right and bear left along the field-edge. Follow marker posts steeply downhill, bearing right through grassland and parallel with a fence on your right, to reach a gate within woodland. Continue straight on and soon turn right along a track. Descend steeply and soon bear left on to the track through Ashcombe Bottom. Keep right and pass Ashcombe Farm.

In 1930 the photographer, designer, painter and writer Sir Cecil Beaton (1904–80) rented Ashcombe House. He is buried in Broad Chalke in the neighbouring Ebble Valley.

Where the track bears right uphill at Point Ⓒ, keep straight on. Follow the path in front of a cottage, continuing through a gate and along the valley bottom. As the track curves right to a gate at Point Ⓓ, bear off left through a waymarked kissing gate, go through a small metal gate, and turn left. Immediately bear right along the signposted track towards Tollard Royal. Continue through a gate back to the pond in the centre of the village.

# Roundway Hill

| | | |
|---|---|---|
| DISTANCE 4.5 miles (7.2km) | MINIMUM TIME 2hrs | |
| ASCENT/GRADIENT 262ft (80m) ▲▲▲ | LEVEL OF DIFFICULTY ✦✦✦ | |

PATHS Tracks, field paths, stretches of road

LANDSCAPE High chalk downland

SUGGESTED MAP OS Explorer 157 Marlborough & Savernake Forest

START/FINISH Grid reference: SU013639

DOG FRIENDLINESS Can be off lead along tracks, but under control on farmland

PARKING Car park by The Plantation north of Roundway village

PUBLIC TOILETS None on route

Roundway Hill forms a wide ridge of high chalk downland below the summits of Beacon Hill, King's Play Hill and Morgan's Hill, which rise steeply out of the Avon Valley north of Devizes. Now a peaceful scene of wide-open fields and grassy scarp slopes, this breezy, unspoilt downland once rang with the sound of battle cries. On 13 July 1643, a small Royalist army defeated the Parliamentarians in a bloody skirmish that killed more than 600 troops and saw 1,200 wounded or captured.

## THE LOBSTERS

It was following an indecisive battle at Lansdown near Bath that the Parliamentarian army, led by Sir William Waller, pursued a weakened Royalist army and their blinded leader Lord Hopton to Devizes where they had occupied the castle and barricaded the streets. Weary, short of ammunition and aware than an unfortified Devizes would not withstand a siege for long, Hopton sent Prince Maurice to Oxford for reinforcements. Knowing that Hopton's cavalry were in bad shape, yet unaware that Prince Maurice had escaped from Devizes, Waller took his time in besieging the town as his troops needed rest following the Battle of Lansdown. Eventually, news that Prince Maurice and Lord Wilmot were returning to Devizes with three brigades of cavalry (2,000 men), forced Waller to rally his troops on Roundway Down. Waller sent out his cavalry, known as 'The Lobsters', to meet Wilmot's brigade and it was here that the two mounted armies clashed. Wilmot's troopers charged twice and forced the Parliamentarians west towards Oliver's Castle. Waller's infantry was unable to fire at the Royalists for fear of hitting their own men.

## BLOODY DITCH

The fleeing Parliamentarian cavalry, unaware of the steep scarp slope on the other side of Oliver's Castle, was chased to the edge and forced down the slope. Many men and horses broke their necks as they plunged over the 300ft (91m) precipice. Others were killed by the newly arrived Royalist infantry who had sallied forth from Devizes on hearing a prearranged gun signal from Lord Wilmot. Since then, this combe has been known as Bloody Ditch, and skeletons and military equipment are still occasionally found here.

Wilmot's cavalry returned to attack Waller's infantry, who fought on bravely, but seeing the 2,000 Royalist troops rising over Roundway Down from Devizes, they broke and fled, and many were cut down by the victorious Royalists. The hill was subsequently named Runaway Hill by the Royalists, and this later became Roundway. The defeat of a superior balanced army in proper battle order by a column of cavalry that had ridden down from Oxford was regarded as a remarkable event. As a result of this loss, Waller was unable to replace the Earl of Wessex as Lord General of the Parliamentarian army. Also, with no Parliamentary forces left in the West Country, the Royalists had won an important victory.

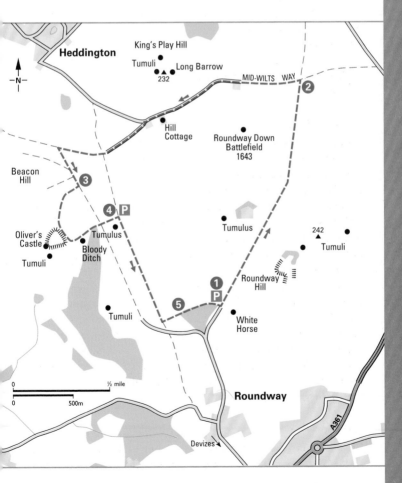

# FLORA AND FAUNA ON ROUNDWAY HILL

The wooded area close to the walk's start and finish includes several open grassy areas. Here you can enjoy the views and admire the chalk-loving plants and the wide variety of insects as you stroll among the trees. Butterflies, grasshoppers and bees are known to inhabit this corner of Roundway Hill.

**1** From the parking area take the track across Roundway Hill for 1.25 miles (2km), heading north towards masts on the horizon. Along this stretch the track's surface is good and firm underfoot. Swing slightly left to pass the Civil War battle site.

**2** At a crossing of tracks, turn left along a track, following the Mid-Wilts Way. Pass a barn on the left and then in 0.5 miles (800m), at Hill Cottage, fork left. Where the track swings left, keep straight on along a narrow, rutted and often muddy track. Gently ascend and, near the summit, turn sharp left on the Mid-Wilts Way, keeping straight ahead between two fields, with excellent views unfolding to your right.

**3** Follow the Mid-Wilts Way through a gate on the right and maintain the same direction, heading down the slope and round to the right in the field corner. Make for a kissing gate, keep left and follow the path around the top of the escarpment and around Oliver's Castle, eventually reaching the steep combe known as Bloody Ditch. Walk to the left of woodland to reach a parking area.

**4** Turn right at the track, then almost immediately left, avoiding the Mid-Wilts Way on the right. In 200yds (183m), where the track swings left, turn right and walk along the left-hand field-edge. Gradually ascend and in the top corner, turn left into a wooded enclosure.

**5** Keep ahead, passing along the edge of the wood and soon merge with a track. Continue ahead and beyond the trees you reach the car park above Roundway village where the walk began.

WHERE TO EAT AND DRINK  Take a packed lunch to the picnic site above Bloody Ditch or find a pub in one of the many nearby villages.

WHAT TO SEE  At the end of the walk, view the newest of the Wiltshire White Horses, the Millennium White Horse, which was cut into Roundway Down in 1999 to replace the 1845 White Horse that had become overgrown. Close by is another Wiltshire chalk horse – the 1780 Cherhill Horse, near Calne. This is the work of Dr Alsop, who is said to have stood more than a mile (1.6km) from his workmen, shouting instructions through a megaphone.

WHILE YOU'RE THERE  Visit Devizes Museum to see the Civil War weapons found on Roundway Down and read the collection of original pamphlets describing the Civil War battles and sieges.

# Great Chalfield from Holt

| | |
|---|---|
| DISTANCE 3 miles (4.8km) | MINIMUM TIME 1hr 30min |

ASCENT/GRADIENT 147ft (45m) ▲▲▲    LEVEL OF DIFFICULTY ✦✦✦

PATHS Field paths, metalled track, country lanes

LANDSCAPE Gently undulating farmland

SUGGESTED MAP AA Leisure Map 15 Swindon & Devizes

START/FINISH Grid reference: ST861619

DOG FRIENDLINESS Keep dogs under control at all times

PARKING Holt Village Hall car park (visitors to The Courts only) or on street in Holt

PUBLIC TOILETS Only if visiting The Courts or Great Chalfield Manor

Holt is a rare industrial Wiltshire village with a significant history as a cloth-making and leather-tanning centre. The tannery, founded in the early 18th century, still occupies the main three-storey factory in the appropriately named small industrial area – The Midlands – while bedding manufacture and light engineering now occupy former cloth factories. Holt also enjoyed short-lived fame between 1690 and 1750 as a spa, based on the curative properties of a spring, but its popularity declined in the face of competition from nearby Bath. The most attractive part of the village is at Ham Green, where elegant 17th- and 18th-century houses stand along three sides of a fine green shaded by horse chestnut trees, and a quiet lane leads to the late Victorian parish church with a Perpendicular tower.

## THE COURTS – WILTSHIRE'S SECRET GARDEN

From the green a walled walk leads to The Courts, a substantial 18th-century house that served, as its name suggests, as the place where the local magistrate sat to adjudicate in the disputes of the cloth weavers from Bradford-on-Avon. Although not open, the house makes an attractive backdrop to 7 acres (2.8ha) of authentic English country garden owned by the National Trust. Hidden away behind high walls and reached through an avenue of pleached limes, you will find a series of garden 'rooms'. Stroll along a network of stone paths through formal gardens featuring yew topiary, lawns with colourful herbaceous borders, a lake and a lily pond with aquatic and water-tolerant plants, and explore an area given over to wild flowers among an interesting small arboretum of trees and shrubs.

## GREAT CHALFIELD MANOR

You will glimpse the Tudor chimneys and gabled windows of this enchanting manor house as you stride across peaceful field paths a mile (1.6km) or so northwest of Holt. Enhanced by a moat and gatehouse, this exquisite group of buildings will certainly live up to your expectations and really must be visited. Built by Thomas Tropenell in 1480 during the Wars of the Roses, Great Chalfield is one of the most perfect examples of the late medieval English manor house. Sensitively restored in the early 20th century by Sir Harold Brakspear after two centuries of neglect and disrepair, the manor house is centred on its traditional great hall, which rises to the rafters and is lit by windows, including two beautiful oriels, positioned high in the walls. Join one of the guided tours and you will be able to see the fine vaulting, the chimney place of the hall, the concealed spy-holes in the gallery designed to allow people to see what was going on in the great hall, and the amusing ornaments, gargoyles and other fascinating details of this fine building.

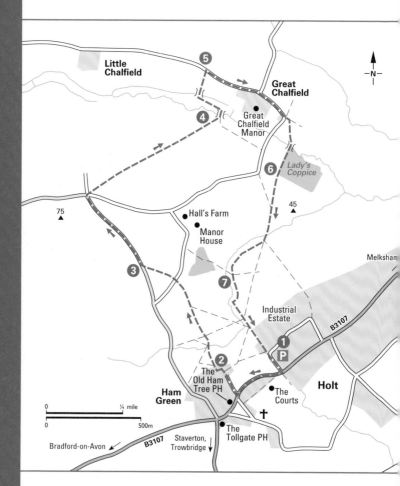

**1** Turn left out of the car park and then right along the B3107 through the village. Just before The Old Ham Tree pub, turn right along Ground Corner. At the end of the lane take the waymarked path left along a drive. Bear right and follow the fenced path beside Highfields to a kissing gate.

**2** Keep to the right along the edge of the field, then keep ahead in the next field towards the clump of fir trees. Continue following the worn path to the right, into a further field. Keep left along the field-edge to a stile in the top corner, maintain direction to a gate and cross the metalled drive and stile opposite. Bear diagonally left through the field to a stile level with the clump of trees to your right, then turn immediately left over a hidden stile in the hedge to a lane.

**3** Turn right along the lane. At a junction, turn right towards Great Chalfield and go through the kissing gate almost immediately on your left. Take the arrowed path right, diagonally across a large field towards Great Chalfield Manor, visible ahead.

**4** Go through a kissing gate and bear half right down to a gate. Cross a footbridge over a stream, go through a gate and bear diagonally left across the field to another bridge. Cross it and go ahead beside the hedge to a metalled track by a barn.

**5** Turn right, then right again when you reach the lane, passing in front of Great Chalfield Manor. At the sharp right-hand bend, go through the gate ahead and bear right across a field. Cross a footbridge over a stream and walk straight on up a field beside woodland to a kissing gate in the corner.

**6** Cross a track and follow the left-hand field-edge to a kissing gate, then follow the path straight ahead towards a chimney on the skyline. Go through a gate, bear immediately right to a gate in the hedge and turn right along the path around the field-edge.

**7** Ignore the stile on your right and continue to the field corner and a raised path beside water. Go through a gate and turn left along the field-edge to a further gate on your left. Join the drive past Garland Farm and pass between small factory buildings to the road. Turn right, back to the car park.

WHERE TO EAT AND DRINK You will find a choice of pubs in Holt. The 16th-century Tollgate offers innovative, freshly produced food on varied menus alongside fine wines and local ales. For more traditional pub food head for The Old Ham Tree, which overlooks the green.

WHAT TO SEE A huge factory dominates the landscape south of Holt at Staverton, standing beside the River Avon. The building dates from 1824. All that remains of Holt Spa is an arch, pump handle and stone tablet on one of the factory walls in the industrial estate.

WHILE YOU'RE THERE Visit Trowbridge Museum in Home Mill, the town's last working woollen mill, and learn more about the woollen mills and cloth-making industry of the Avon Valley in West Wiltshire.

# Castle Combe and By Brook

| | |
|---|---|
| DISTANCE 5.75 miles (9.2km) | MINIMUM TIME 2hrs 30min |

ASCENT/GRADIENT 515ft (157m) ▲▲▲  LEVEL OF DIFFICULTY ✦✦✦

PATHS Field and woodland paths and tracks, metalled lanes, several stiles

LANDSCAPE Wooded river valley and village streets

SUGGESTED MAP AA Leisure Map 15 Swindon & Devizes

START/FINISH Grid reference: ST845776

DOG FRIENDLINESS Keep under control across pasture and golf course

PARKING Free car park just off B4039 at Upper Castle Combe

PUBLIC TOILETS Castle Combe

Since being voted 'the prettiest village in England' in 1962, there have been more visitors to Castle Combe, more photographs taken of it and more words written about it than any other village in the county. Nestling deep in a steam-threaded combe, just a mile (1.6km) from the M4, you'll find 15th-century Cotswold stone cottages with steep gabled roofs surrounding a turreted church and stone-canopied market cross, a medieval manor house, a fast-flowing steam in the main street leading to an ancient packhorse bridge, and a perfectly picturesque river.

Yet, as preservation is taken so seriously here, a palpable atmosphere of unreality surrounds this tiny 'toytown', where television aerials don't exist, gardens are immaculately kept, and the inevitable commercialism is carefully concealed. Behind this present-day facade, however, exists a fascinating history that's well worth exploring, and the timeless valleys and tumbling wooded hillsides that surround the village are favourite Wiltshire walking destinations. If you don't like crowds and really want to enjoy Castle Combe, undertake this walk on a winter weekday.

### 'CASTLECOMBE' CLOTH

The castle, which gave the village its name, of which little more than earthworks remain, began life as a Roman fort and was used by the Saxons before becoming a Norman castle in 1135 and the home of the de Dunstanville family. In the 13th and 14th centuries the village established itself as an important weaving centre. With the growth of the cloth trade in Wiltshire, Castle Combe prospered, becoming more like a town, with a weekly market and annual fair.

The greatest tribute to the wealth of the weaving industry is reflected in St Andrew's Church. Its impressive Perpendicular tower was built in 1436. For centuries the villages produced a red-and-white cloth known as Castlecombe. Cloth manufacture began to decline in the early 18th century when the diminutive By Brook was unable to power the larger machinery. People moved to the larger towns and Castle Combe became depopulated and returned to an agricultural existence. An annual fair, centred around the Market Cross, continued until 1904, and Castle Combe remained an 'estate' village until 1947 when the village was sold at auction.

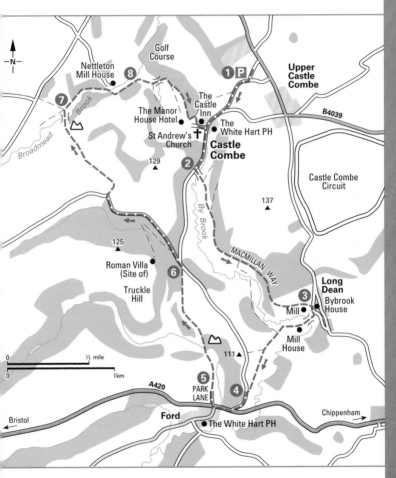

**1** Leave the car park via the steps and turn right. At the T-junction, turn right again and follow the lane into Castle Combe. Keep left at the Market Cross, then cross the By Brook and continue along the road. Take the waymarked path across the bridge on your left.

**2** Pass through a gate and follow the path uphill and then beside the right-hand fence above the valley (Macmillan Way). Beyond an open area, wind gently through woodland to a stone stile and gate. Cross a further stile and descend into the hamlet of Long Dean.

**3** Where the lane bears left by Bybrook House, follow the track right to cross the river bridge. At a mill house, keep right and follow the sunken bridleway uphill to a gate. Shortly enter sloping pasture and follow the enclosed path around the top edge. Bear left across a stile to follow a worn path through the field to a stile and lane.

**4** Turn left and descend to the A420 at Ford. Turn right along the pavement and shortly turn right again into Park Lane. (If you want to visit The White Hart in Ford village, take the road ahead on your left, signed 'Colerne'.) Climb the gravel track and take the footpath left through a gate.

**5** Keep right through pasture and continue through trees to a water-meadow in the valley bottom. Turn left, follow the path to a stile and cross a stream. Steeply ascend the grassy slope ahead of you, bearing left beyond some trees towards a waymarker post. Follow the footpath along the top of the field to a stile

and gate, then walk through the woodland to a gate and the road.

**6** Turn left at the immediate fork. Keep to the road for 0.5 miles (800m) and take the arrowed bridleway, right, on a sharp left-hand bend. Follow the track, then, just before a gate, keep right downhill on a sunken path to come to a footbridge over Broadmead Brook.

**7** In 20yds (18m), cross the remains of a stile on your right and follow the footpath close to the river. Cross another stile and soon pass beside Nettleton Mill House, bearing right to a hidden gate. Walk beside the stream, cross a stile and enter a golf course.

**8** Turn right along the metalled track, cross the bridge and turn immediately right again. After 50yds (46m) bear left to follow a parallel path running below the golf course fairway. Walk beside a wall to reach a stile on your right. Drop down to a metalled drive and keep ahead back into Castle Combe. Turn left at the Market Cross and retrace your steps.

**WHERE TO EAT AND DRINK** The White Hart at Ford is the perfect halfway refuelling stop. Expect excellent real ales, interesting bar food and a riverside garden. In Castle Combe, head for another White Hart in a part-timbered 14th-century building for cosy log fires, a summer patio garden and an extensive pub menu. Across the road, The Castle Inn Hotel offers a more contemporary menu. The impressive Manor House Hotel is the place for afternoon teas.

**WHAT TO SEE** St Andrew's Church in Castle Combe is worth closer inspection. On the parapet, note the 50 stone heads and the carving of a shuttle and scissors, the mark of the cloth industry put there by merchants who built the church. Inside, don't miss the rare faceless clock made by a local blacksmith in 1380, and the 13th-century tomb of Sir Walter de Dunstanville. Along the By Brook, note the former fulling mills and weavers' cottages at the remote and unspoilt hamlet of Long Dean.

**WHILE YOU'RE THERE** Linger by the bridge over the By Brook and recall, if you've seen it, the 1966 film *Dr Doolittle*. Although miles from the coast, a jetty was built on the banks in front of the 17th-century cottages here to create a fishing harbour, complete with seven boats and plastic cobbles. In 2010 Steven Spielberg shot part of his epic movie *Warhorse* in Castle Combe.

*Right: Castle Combe (Walk 37)*

# Around Lacock

DISTANCE 5.5 miles (8.8km)   MINIMUM TIME 2hrs 30min

ASCENT/GRADIENT 426ft (130m) ▲▲▲   LEVEL OF DIFFICULTY ✦✦✦

PATHS Field paths and tracks; some road walking, many stiles

LANDSCAPE River valley, wooded hillside and parkland

SUGGESTED MAP AA Leisure Map 15 Swindon & Devizes

START/FINISH Grid reference: ST918682

DOG FRIENDLINESS Dogs can be off lead on riverside pastures if free of cattle

PARKING Car park on edge of Lacock (free for National Trust members)

PUBLIC TOILETS Adjacent to The Stables tea room in Lacock village

Timeless Lacock, packed with attractive buildings from the 13th to 18th centuries, possesses all the character and atmosphere of medieval England. Half-timbering, lichen grey stone, red-brick and whitewashed facades crowd together and above eye-level, uneven upper storeys, gabled ends and stone roofs blend with charming ease.

With the founding of an abbey in the 13th century, the village grew rich on the medieval wool industry and continued to prosper as an important coaching stop between Marlborough and Bristol until the mid-18th century when, as an estate-owned village, time seemed to stand still for nearly 100 years. Owned and preserved by the National Trust since 1944, Lacock is among England's most beautiful villages and is one of Wiltshire's most visited.

## FOX TALBOT AND LACOCK ABBEY

Lacock Abbey, on the outskirts, began as an Augustinian nunnery in 1232, but after the Reformation Sir William Sharrington used the remains to build a Tudor mansion, preserving the fine cloister court, sacristy and chapter house, and adding a romantic octagonal tower, courtyard and chimney stacks.

The abbey passed to the Talbot family through marriage and they Gothicised the south elevation and added the oriel windows. This was the setting for the experiments of William Henry Fox Talbot (1800–77), which in 1835 led to the creation of the world's first photographic negative. You can see some of Fox Talbot's work and equipment, alongside photographic exhibitions, in the 16th-century barn at the gates to the abbey.

## VILLAGE HIGHLIGHTS

Architectural gems to note as you wander around Lacock's ancient streets include the timber-framed inn At the Sign of the Angel, on Church Street, which retains its medieval layout, a 16th-century doorway and the passage through which horses would pass. Nearby Cruck House, with one of its cruck beams exposed, is a rare example of this 14th-century building method. Further along is King Johns Hunting Lodge, reputed to be even older than the abbey, and St Cyriac's Church, which contains the grandiose Renaissance tomb of Sir William Sharrington. In West Street, The George Inn dates back to 1361 and features a huge open fire with a dogwheel, which was connected to the spit on the fire and turned by a dog called a Turnspit. Next door to the pub take a quick look at the bus shelter; it was formerly the village smithy.

On the corner of East Street is a magnificent 14th-century tithe barn with fine curved timbers. It later became the market hall. Finally, don't miss the 18th-century domed lock-up next door. This is known as a 'blind house', since many of its overnight prisoners were drunks. You may recognise Lacock's medieval streets as the backdrop to several television costume dramas, notably Jane Austen's *Pride and Prejudice* (1995) and *Emma* (1996), and Daniel Defoe's bawdy *Moll Flanders* (1996).

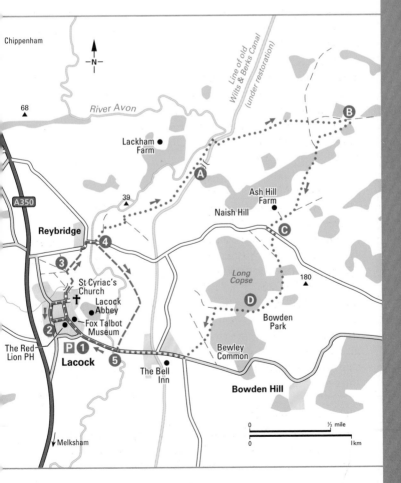

➊ From the car park entrance, cross the road and follow the gravel path into the village, passing the entrance to Lacock Abbey and the Fox Talbot Museum. Turn right into East Street opposite The Red Lion and walk down to Church Street. Turn left, pass At the Sign of the Angel with its magnificent 16th-century doorway and bear left into West Street to opposite The George Inn. Shortly, follow the road left into High Street.

➋ Pass the National Trust shop and turn left to walk back down East Street. Turn right along Church Street and bear left in front of St Cyriac's Church to cross an ancient packhorse bridge over the Bide Brook. Follow the path by the stream, then up the lane to reach the end of the road.

➌ Go through the kissing gate on your right and follow the tarmac path across the field to another kissing gate. Pass the stone cottages at Reybridge to a lane. Turn right along the lane and then right again to cross the River Avon.

➍ Immediately cross the stile on your right and bear diagonally left to the far corner where you rejoin the riverbank to reach a kissing gate. Walk beside the river for 200yds (183m) to a stile, and cross the field following the line of electricity poles to a gate. Keep straight on to a stile beside a gate, and then head towards the stone bridge over the Avon.

➎ Climb the stile and turn right across the bridge. Join the raised pavement and follow it back into the village and car park.

WHERE TO EAT AND DRINK You are spoilt for choice in Lacock. For snacks and lunches head for the National Trust's Stables tea room or King Johns Hunting Lodge; for pub lunches try The Red Lion, The George Inn or The Carpenters Arms. For a treat try the At the Sign of the Angel restaurant.

WHAT TO SEE In Lacock, look for the print of Fox Talbot's first photographic negative, showing a detail of the abbey and its oriel window. Explore the cloister court and adjoining rooms and see where many scenes from *Harry Potter and the Philosopher's Stone* (2001) were filmed.

WHILE YOU'RE THERE Just to the north of Lacock is Lackham Farm. Here you will find historic barns and granaries housing an intriguing range of displays depicting Wiltshire agriculture and rural life. There are also attractive walled gardens and an animal trail.

# Bowden Park

DISTANCE 5.5 miles (8.8km)   MINIMUM TIME 2hrs 30min

ASCENT/GRADIENT 426ft (130m) ▲▲▲   LEVEL OF DIFFICULTY ✦✦✦

SEE MAP AND INFORMATION PANEL FOR WALK 38

From Point ❹ of Walk 38, climb the stile on your left and turn right along the field-edge. Follow the path through scrub to a stile and proceed ahead to cross another stile on to a tarmac path beside the old Wilts and Berks Canal.

The canal was opened in 1810 and linked Semington, on the Kennet and Avon Canal, to Abingdon and the Thames in Oxfordshire, a distance of 51 miles (82km) with 42 locks. Coal from Somerset was the main cargo until the canal was formally abandoned in 1914.

Pass a restored bridge at Point ❹; then take the first footpath on the right, across the canal to a gate. Follow the canal left, along the bottom edge of a field, to a stile. Climb through trees and scrub to a stile, then follow the worn path ahead and along the field-edge to a gate. Cross the next field to a gate, then keep ahead to cross a metalled farm drive and continue along the field-edge to a gate. Ascend a grassy track to a gate and walk uphill towards a house. Before a gate, turn right across the top of the field, passing below a second house to a gate on the far side, Point ❸. Continue ahead to a farm drive, then turn left and ascend through woodland. Carry on up the hill to a gate and continue to a lane.

Turn left, then cross the stile on the right before a house, Point ❹. Keep to the left-hand edge of the field, crossing an electric fence over an insulator 'stile'. Cross a stile and second electric fence and bear diagonally left to a third fence and stile in the field corner. Cross the stile ahead into woodland and continue to another stile. Go ahead along the field-edge to a stile on your right. Bear half left across Bowden Park, keeping right of a clump of trees. Bear right, downhill along the field-edge, to a stile beside a gate, Point ❹.

Head downhill to a stile and turn left around the field-edge to a stile and gate near a house. Follow the path to the drive and follow it left. After passing between hedges, bear right on to a worn path across Bewley Common to the road. Turn right and return to Lacock.

# Malmesbury and the Avon

DISTANCE 2 miles (3.2km)    MINIMUM TIME 1hr

ASCENT/GRADIENT 49ft (15m) ▲▲▲    LEVEL OF DIFFICULTY ✛✛✛

PATHS Field paths, town streets

LANDSCAPE River valley and urban area

SUGGESTED MAP OS Explorer 168 Stroud, Tetbury & Malmesbury

START/FINISH Grid reference: ST932875

DOG FRIENDLINESS No problems on riverside pastures

PARKING Station Road pay car park, Malmesbury

PUBLIC TOILETS Malmesbury town centre

Malmesbury stands between two branches of the River Avon on the site of a Saxon fortified hilltop town. Much of the walk is within Malmesbury. Dominating the surviving medieval street plan are the remains of a Benedictine abbey, founded in the 7th century AD by St Aldhelm, its first abbot. Malmesbury is one of the oldest boroughs in England, the original royal charter was granted by King Alfred in AD 880 and confirmed by King Athelstan (reigned AD 925–939), when he made Malmesbury his capital, holding court just outside of the town.

## KILLED BY A TIGER

Outside the abbey is the famous grave of Hannah Twynnoy, who died in 1703, aged 33. She was killed by a tiger, which was part of a menagerie visiting the town. After the dissolution of the monasteries in the 1540s, the abbey was sold for £1,517 to local wool merchant William Stumpe, who presented the surviving nave to the townspeople for their parish church. In the following centuries several mills sprang up along the local rivers and the town became an important centre for the manufacture of woollen cloth. It later became renowned for producing fine lace and silk.

## BURGESSES AND COMMONERS

Among many historic landmarks visited on this walk is Abbey House, a handsome Tudor building built by William Stumpe in the mid-16th century on monastic foundations. It has a 5-acre (2ha) garden featuring one of Britain's largest private collections of roses.  Also part of the trail is St John's Street, which has many ancient houses, including a collection of almshouses from 1694 built on the site of St John the Baptist's Hospital. Incorporated in the gable wall is an early 13th-century arch. The Old Courthouse, through School Arch, is where the Old Corporation of Burgesses and Commoners have met since 1616. These are direct descendants of the men living in Malmesbury more than 1,000 years ago to whom King Athelstan gave 500 acres (202.5ha) of common land (King's Heath) for their help in the battle against the Danes, and this land is still passed down the generations.

## THE TOMB OF KING ATHELSTAN

One of Malmesbury's most famous landmarks is the 500-year-old Market Cross, an elaborate, octagonal building with intricate carvings, built for the market traders to stand in when wet. The isolated steeple is the remnant of 13th-century St Paul's church, the parish church until 1541. This now serves as the bell tower for the abbey church. Among the more striking features of the abbey are the Norman porch, with its exquisite carvings, the vaulted nave roof, the 14th-century stone screens in the north and south aisles, and the tomb of King Athelstan.

Near the start of the walk is Conygre Mead Nature Reserve, which is rich in wildlife and includes 170 plant species, 18 types of butterfly and various breeding birds. On the slopes grow native wild flowers such as common knapweed. In 1993 a pond close to the river here was re-excavated for the benefit of wildlife.

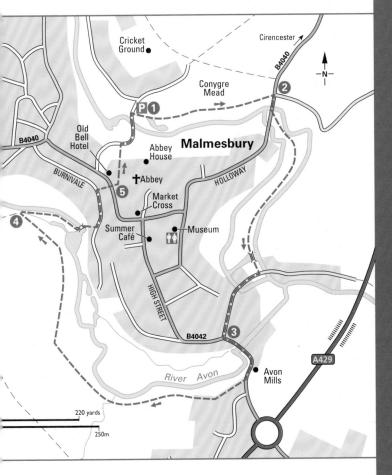

**1** From the car park, keep the river to your right and walk towards the abbey and Abbey House. At the information board, bear left, then right through a kissing gate into Conygre Mead. Keep right along the path and walk along the riverbank, noting the old railway tunnel and Abbey House across the river.

**2** At the road turn right across the bridge and descend steps to reach a stile. Keep right across Longmead to the remains of a railway line in the right-hand field corner. Take the left-hand path through the next field and walk along the riverbank to a stile and footbridge. Cross the old sluice gate and continue to the lane beside Wynyard Mill. Turn right past the bowls club, following St John's Street to Lower High Street.

**3** Cross the road and go through the memorial gates and bear left along the walkway parallel to St John's Bridge to rejoin the road opposite Avon Mills. Turn right along the pavement and go through the gate on your right to follow the permissive path beside the River Avon. Cross a stile and keep to the path through gates and across various footbridges, soon to leave the river, keeping beside the hedge to a gap in the field corner and a small stone bridge.

**4** Cross the bridge where the path becomes paved to reach a footbridge across the Avon. At a T-junction, turn left along Burnivale, then climb Betty Geezers Steps on your right to reach Abbey Row, with the Civic Trust Garden on your left. Cross the road and bear right in front of the Old Bell Hotel and enter the close to visit the abbey.

**5** Return to the Old Bell and take the path immediately right for the Cloister Garden. Walk through the garden and turn left down steps, then right along Mill Lane back to the car park.

**WHERE TO EAT AND DRINK** Try the Summer Café for tasty snacks and lunches. Excellent coffee, afternoon teas and light lunches are also served in the Old Bell Hotel near the walk's start and finish point.

**WHAT TO SEE** Locate the stained-glass window in the abbey commemorating Brother Elmer, an 11th-century monk, who once tried to fly from the abbey's west tower. Having fastened home-made wings to his feet and hands he jumped and flew some 600ft (183m) before crashing, breaking both legs and laming himself.

**WHILE YOU'RE THERE** Explore the old streets and visit Athelstan Museum in the Town Hall in Cross Hayes. Inside is a fascinating mix of displays, including Malmesbury's first fire engine and the story of the Abbey.

*Right: Bluebells near Malmesbury (Walk 40)*

# The Fosse Way from Sherston and Easton Grey

| | |
|---|---|
| DISTANCE 6.5 miles (10.4km) | MINIMUM TIME 3hrs |

ASCENT/GRADIENT 131ft (40m) ▲▲▲     LEVEL OF DIFFICULTY ✦✦✦

PATHS Field and parkland paths, tracks, metalled lanes, many stiles

LANDSCAPE River valley and gently rolling farmland

SUGGESTED MAP AA Leisure Map 15 Swindon & Devizes

START/FINISH Grid reference: ST853858

DOG FRIENDLINESS Dogs can be off lead along Fosse Way

PARKING Sherston High Street; plenty of roadside parking

PUBLIC TOILETS None on route

The Bristol Avon rises in the foothills of the Cotswolds in the northwest corner of Wiltshire and is little more than a wide and shallow stream as it flows through the countryside west of Malmesbury. Despite its size, the river enhances all the charming little stone villages in this unspoilt and somewhat forgotten area of north Wiltshire, which is typically Cotswold in appearance and character. In fact, 18 villages between Colerne and Malmesbury are officially part of the Cotswold Area of Outstanding Natural Beauty. Of these, Sherston must rank among the most attractive, with its wide High Street lined with some interesting 17th- and 18th-century buildings. It prospered as a result of the flourishing wool trade at the time and still has the feel of a market town.

## LEGEND OF A LOCAL HERO

It has been suggested that Sherston is Sceorstan, as chronicled by Henry of Huntingdon, where in 1016 Edmund Ironside won a battle against the Danes led by King Canute. The early legend of John Rattlebone, a local yeoman promised land by Ironside in return for service against the Danes, is deep rooted. This brave knight was terribly wounded in battle and although he staunched his bleeding and continued fighting, he reputedly died as Canute's army withdrew. Other traditions say he survived to claim his reward.

It is said that the small stone effigy on the south side of the porch outside the parish church is that of Rattlebone, and that an ancient timber chest in the church, marked with the initials RB, is supposed to be where he kept his armour. Whatever the truth is, the Rattlebone Inn opposite the church keeps his name alive.

## EASTON GREY – PURE COTSWOLD CHARM

Peaceful parkland and riverside paths lead you downstream to picturesque Easton Grey. Set around a 16th-century stone bridge and climbing a short, curving street is an intimate huddle of ancient stone houses, with mullioned windows, steep, lichen-covered roofs and colourful, flower-filled gardens that touch the riverbank. Set back on a rise above the river is Easton Grey House, a handsome 18th-century manor house with a classical facade and portico, surrounded by elegant gardens and lovely valley views. It was the summer retreat of Herbert Asquith, 1st Earl of Oxford, when he was prime minister between 1908 and 1916.

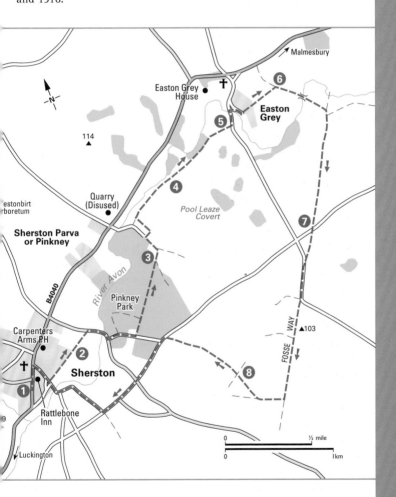

❶ On Sherton's High Street, walk towards the village stores, pass the Rattlebone Inn and turn right into Noble Street. Pass Grove Road and take the footpath left up a flight of steps. Cross a cul-de-sac and follow the metalled footpath to a gate. Continue at the rear of houses to a further gate.

**2** Bear slightly right across a field to a stile, then on to a kissing gate leading out to a lane. Turn right, cross the river and turn immediately left. At the end of woodland on your left, take the footpath left through a gate. Follow the track across Pinkney Park to a gate.

**3** Keep ahead, bearing left beside the wall to a gate. Immediately beyond it turn right for a few paces, then left through a gate. Follow the path right around the edge of a field to a stile. Cross it, then go immediately right over the adjacent stile. Aim for the left-hand corner of the field to the next stile. Keep alongside the fence to the next stile and bear right to a gate.

**4** Bear diagonally left across the field (Easton Grey House is visible in the distance) to a stile in the far corner. Cross a footbridge to a second stile and keep ahead along the left-hand edge of a field. At the end, join a track downhill to a gate and lane.

**5** Turn left into Easton Grey. Cross the river bridge and turn right uphill. With entrance gates ahead, bear left on to a footpath across a gravelled parking area to an unmarked field gate. Go through and keep ahead to a stile. Maintain direction across the next field and gently descend to follow a track into the next field.

**6** Turn right along the field-edge and bear off right in the corner, downhill through scrub to a footbridge. Keep ahead beside a ruin and cross a grassy area to a kissing gate. Continue to a stile and gate and follow the track downhill to a junction with a wider track – the Fosse Way. Turn right and continue for just over 0.5 miles (around 900m) to a road.

**7** Cross straight over and follow the byway to another road. Bear left and keep ahead where the lane veers sharp left. Follow this track for around 0.5 miles (800m), as far as the second footpath on the right. Cross the arrowed stile and follow the grassy path ahead between paddocks, then go over a stile ahead and continue along the right-hand edge of a field until a gateway on the right. Go through and turn immediately left, walking between the hedge and a paddock fence and on to a track.

**8** Skirt to the left of a racehorse gallop, through the narrow gap between a barrier and conifer hedge to a field gate. Walk through scrub to another gate and follow the track ahead to a road. Turn left and continue to a crossroads. Proceed straight on to the next junction and keep ahead, following the lane all the way back into Sherston.

WHERE TO EAT AND DRINK Rest and refuel at the lively Rattlebone Inn in Sherston. The rambling bars are the setting for hearty lunchtime snacks and imaginative evening meals with decent wine and Youngs ales. Alternatively, try the Carpenters Arms, which is noted for its fish.

WHAT TO SEE The wide, hedged, straight track you follow on your return to Sherston is the Fosse Way. This ancient Roman road ran from Lincoln to Exeter and is so named because it was bordered on both sides by a 'fosse' or ditch.

WHILE YOU'RE THERE Nearby Luckington Court Gardens has a 3-acre (1.2ha) formal garden and a walled flower garden. Head north just across the border into Gloucestershire to visit Westonbirt Arboretum, one of the finest and most important collections of trees and shrubs in the country.

# Brunel's Great Tunnel Through Box Hill

| | |
|---|---|
| DISTANCE 3.25 miles (5.3km) | MINIMUM TIME 1hr 45min |
| ASCENT/GRADIENT 508ft (155m) ▲▲▲ | LEVEL OF DIFFICULTY ✦✦✦ |

PATHS Field and woodland paths, bridleways, lanes, many stiles

LANDSCAPE River valley and wooded hillsides

SUGGESTED MAP AA Walker's Map 25 Bristol, Bath & The Mendips

START/FINISH Grid reference: ST824686

DOG FRIENDLINESS Can be off lead on Box Hill Common and in woodland

PARKING Village car park near Selwyn Hall

PUBLIC TOILETS Sports pavilion at start

Box is a large straggling village that sits astride the busy A4 in hilly country halfway between Bath and Chippenham. Although stone has been quarried here since the 9th century, Box really found fame during the 18th century when the local stone was used for Bath's magnificent buildings. The construction of Box Tunnel uncovered immense deposits of good stone and by 1900 Box stone quarries were among the most productive in the world. Little trace can be seen above ground today, except for some fine stone-built houses in the village and a few reminders on Box Hill.

## BRUNEL'S FAMOUS TUNNEL

In 1833, the newly created Great Western Railway appointed Isambard Kingdom Brunel (1806–59) as engineer. His task was to build a railway covering the 118 miles (190km) from London to Bristol. After a relatively straightforward and level start through the Home Counties, he came to the hilly Cotswolds.

The solution at Box would be a tunnel; nearly 2 miles (3.2km) long and with a gradient of 1:100 it would be the longest and steepest in the world at the time. It would also be very wide. Brunel ignored the gauge of other companies, preferring the 7ft (2.1m) used by tramways and roads (and, it was believed, Roman chariots). He also made the tunnel dead straight, and, never one to 'hide his light', the alignment was calculated so the dawn sun would shine through on his birthday on 9 April. Unfortunately he did not allow for atmospheric refraction and was two days out!

## PASSAGE TO NARNIA?

All was on a grand scale: a ton of gunpowder and candles were used every week, 3 million bricks were fired to line the soft Cotswold limestone and 100 navvies lost their lives working on the tunnel. After 2.5 years the way was open, and although Brunel would ultimately lose the battle of the gauges, his magnificent line meant that Bristol was then a mere two hours from the capital. Although artificial, like many large dark holes, the tunnel has collected its fair share of mystery with tales of noises, people under the hill and trains entering the tunnel, never to re-emerge. But as is often the case, the explanations are rather more mundane: To test excavation conditions, Brunel dug a small trial section alongside what is now the eastern entrance and the military commandeered this section during World War II as a safe and fairly secret store for ammunition, records and top brass. Sadly it is not a passage to Narnia!

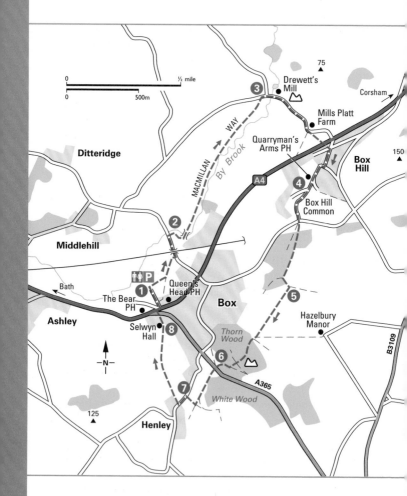

❶ Facing the recreation ground, walk along the left-hand side of the football pitch to join a track in the corner close to the railway line. When you reach the lane, turn left, pass beneath the railway, cross a bridge and take the arrowed footpath to the right, before the second bridge.

② Walk beside the river, cross a footbridge and turn right. Cross a further footbridge and continue to a kissing gate. Walk through water-meadows close to the river, go through a gate and maintain direction. Shortly, bear left to a kissing gate in the field corner. Follow the right-hand field-edge to a kissing gate and lane.

③ Turn right, then right again at the junction. Cross the river, pass Drewett's Mill and steeply ascend the lane. Just past Mills Platt Farm, where there are two rights of way, take the left-hand path up to a stile. Continue steeply uphill to a stile and cross the A4. Ascend steps to a lane and proceed straight on up Barnetts Hill. Keep right at the fork, then right again and pass the Quarryman's Arms.

④ Keep left at the fork and continue beside Box Hill Common to a junction. Take the bridleway straight ahead into woodland. Almost immediately, fork left and follow the path close to the woodland edge. As it curves right into the beech wood, bear left and follow the path by the remains of a wall. Maintain the same direction, then bend left to emerge from the trees.

⑤ Turn right through a wooden gate and follow an enclosed path. Turn right at the T-junction and take the path left to a stile. Cross a further stile and descend into Thorn Wood, following the stepped path to a stile at the bottom.

⑥ Continue through scrub to a stile and turn right beside the fence to a wall stile. Bear right to a further stile, then bear left uphill to a stile and the A365. Cross over and follow the drive ahead. Where it curves left, keep ahead along the arrowed path to a house. Climb a few steps, bear right to pass Washwell Cottage and follow the drive uphill to a T-junction.

⑦ Turn left, then on entering Henley, take the path right. Follow the field-edge to a stile, then descend through a paddock to another stile. Continue to a gate.

⑧ Follow the drive ahead, bear left at the garage and take the metalled path right, into Box. Cross the main road and continue to the A4. Turn right, then left down the access road back to Selwyn Hall.

WHERE TO EAT AND DRINK  In Box, you will find both the Queen's Head and The Bear offer good food and ale in convivial surroundings. Time your walk for opening time at the Quarryman's Arms on Box Hill. Enjoy the views across Box from the dining room with a pint of locally brewed ale.

WHAT TO SEE  Explore Box and locate the Blind House on the main street, one of a dozen in Wiltshire for disturbers of the peace. Look for Coleridge House, named after the poet who often broke his journey here on his way to Nether Stowey. Also look for the former Candle Factory on the Rudloe road that once produced the candles used during the building of Box Tunnel, and head east along the A4 for the best view of the tunnel's entrance.

WHILE YOU'RE THERE  Visit Hazelbury Manor at Wadswick (off the B3109) for its restored, richly varied landscaped gardens, with stone and yew circles, a rockery, formal gardens, rose gardens and laburnum walk. Visit the heritage centre in Corsham to learn about the Bath stone quarrying industry.

# Stourhead Estate

DISTANCE 3 miles (4.8km)    MINIMUM TIME 1hr 30min

ASCENT/GRADIENT 262ft (80m) ▲▲▲    LEVEL OF DIFFICULTY ✦✦✦

PATHS Parkland and woodland paths and tracks

LANDSCAPE Woodland and parkland

SUGGESTED MAP OS Explorers 142 Shepton Mallet; 143 Warminster & Trowbridge

START/FINISH Grid reference: ST779340 (on Explorer 142)

DOG FRIENDLINESS Lead required around livestock on White Sheet Hill. Dogs welcome in Stourhead Gardens all day February–October and after 4pm rest of year

PARKING National Trust car park (pay-and-display) at Stourton

PUBLIC TOILETS Stourhead Visitor Centre and Spread Eagle courtyard

Stourton enjoys an idyllic setting in a valley on the edge of the Stourhead Estate. Beautifully preserved, consisting of a pleasing group of 18th-century cottages, an inn, St Peter's Church and a graceful medieval cross, its unique atmosphere is attributable to the glorious views across a lake and one of Europe's finest landscaped parkland gardens. Wealthy banker Henry Hoare acquired Stourhead in 1717. He pulled down medieval Stourton House and commissioned Colen Campbell, the foremost architect and designer of the day, to build a new Palladian-style house. Extended in the 1780s by Sir Richard Colt Hoare, the magnificent interior includes an outstanding Regency library, a significant collection of Chippendale furniture and fine paintings in the elegant gallery.

## A TASTE OF PARADISE

But Stourhead is more famous for its gardens, designed by Henry Hoare II and laid out in four years from 1741. Now National Trust, they are an outstanding example of the English landscape style. Inspired by Italian landscapes and by the artists Claude Lorraine and Nicholas Poussin, Hoare set out to create a poetic landscape at Stourhead. Having dammed the River Stour and diverted the medieval fish ponds to create a large lake, he began his three-dimensional 'painting', planting beech woods to clothe the hills and frame new lakes. Classical temples were located around the central lake at the end of a series of vistas, which change as you stroll around the estate. The gardens are memorable at any time, but in spring the rhododendrons and azaleas are spectacular and the autumnal colours are beautiful.

Along this walk, at Park Hill, you will cross a large bank, formerly the boundary to the original deer park created in 1448 by John Stourton, and pass an Iron Age hill-fort covering 6 acres (2.4ha).

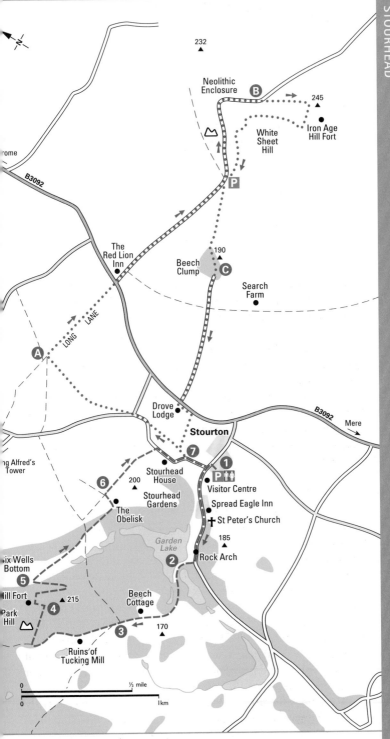

232 ▲

Neolithic
Enclosure **B**

→

245 ▲

White
Sheet
Hill

Iron Age
Hill Fort

⌂

↑

**P**

↓

rome

B3092

→

The
Red Lion
Inn

190 ▲
Beech
Clump **C**

Search
Farm

LONG LANE

→

↓

**A**

Drove
Lodge

B3092

Mere

**Stourton**

←

**7**

**1**
**P** 🚻

ng Alfred's
Tower

Visitor Centre

**6**

200 ▲

Stourhead
House

Spread Eagle Inn

✝ St Peter's Church

Stourhead
Gardens

The
Obelisk

*Garden
Lake*

185 ▲

**2**

ix Wells
Bottom

Rock Arch

**5**

Beech
Cottage

ill Fort

▲ 215

**4**

**3**
←

170 ▲

Park
Hill

⌂

Ruins of
Tucking Mill

0 _____ ½ mile
0 _____ 1 km

❶ Leave the car park via the car exit and turn left down the lane into Stourton village passing the Spread Eagle Inn, St Peter's Church and the entrance to Stourhead Gardens. (Note: National Trust members or those paying to visit the Gardens and Stourhead House can access the village via the visitor centre.) Continue along the lane, pass beneath the Rock Arch and turn immediately right along a track.

❷ Pass beside the lake, cross a cattle grid and follow the track to Beech Cottage. Keep left along the track to a stile beside a gate and ignore the Stour Valley Way signposted to the right. At a fork, bear right through the gate, signed 'Alfred's Tower'.

❸ Proceed ahead on the grassy track along the top of the field to a further gate and stile, noting the ruins of Tucking Mill and cottages on your left. Walk through the woodland and take the first broad track right (by a silver National Trust sign) into coniferous woodland. Ascend steeply to reach Broad Ride at the top, a wide grassy swathe through the woodland.

❹ Turn left to a gate and the Iron Age hill-fort at Park Hill. Do not cross the stile, but bear right along the narrow path beside the fence to reach a track. Turn right and shortly turn sharp left downhill through the woodland to reach a gate at Six Wells Bottom.

❺ Turn right to cross the stile and bear diagonally left across the valley bottom, keeping left of the lake, heading uphill to a gate on the edge of woodland. Continue up the track to a gate and turn immediately left up the bank to pass The Obelisk, with Stourhead House clearly visible now to your right.

❻ On reaching the track, turn right towards Stourhead House. At a junction of tracks, turn right through a gate and pass in front of the house. Walk down the drive and stay on it to reach the gatehouse at the end.

❼ To finish this short loop, pass underneath the gatehouse and turn left up the lane back to the car park. National Trust members and visitors that have paid to enter the Stourhead gardens and house can bear right just before the gatehouse and walk through the walled garden and across a bridge to return to the car park via the visitor centre.

WHERE TO EAT AND DRINK Adjacent to the car park is the National Trust's restaurant serving teas, coffees and light lunches. Alternatively, enjoy a pint and a ploughman's at the Spread Eagle Inn in the village or stop at The Red Lion Inn below White Sheet Hill.

WHILE YOU'RE THERE Don't miss climbing King Alfred's Tower on the edge of the Stourhead Estate (open March to October). This intriguing red-brick folly, built in 1772, stands 160ft (49m) high and affords magnificent views across Somerset, Dorset and Wiltshire.

*Right: King Alfred's Tower on the Stourhead Estate (Walk 43)*

# White Sheet Hill

DISTANCE 5 miles (8km)   MINIMUM TIME 2hrs 30min

ASCENT/GRADIENT 344ft (105m) ▲▲▲   LEVEL OF DIFFICULTY +++

SEE MAP AND INFORMATION PANEL FOR WALK 43

From the gate, Point **7**, beside the main drive follow the path straight across the parkland in front of Stourhead House. Merge with a track and keep ahead through two gates to a lane. Cross the stile opposite and bear half-left across a field to a pair of stiles located between electricity poles. Continue straight ahead to the left of a hedge, following the grass track to a stile in the corner, Point **A**. Drop down steps and turn right along the sunken bridleway (Long Lane) to reach the B3092, opposite the Red Lion Inn. Cross straight over and follow the tarmac lane towards White Sheet Hill. Pass a parking area and continue steeply uphill, following the track sharp right to pass through the neolithic enclosure on White Sheet Hill.

White Sheet Hill is rich in prehistoric monuments, including a rare causewayed enclosure, one of the earliest types of British earthworks. This neolithic camp consists of a ring of short banks and ditches built about 5,500 years ago. Evidence suggests prehistoric local farmers met here for markets, fairs or religious ceremonies, and it was probably not built for defence purposes or to enclose village sites, unlike the high ramparts and deep ditches of the adjacent Iron Age hill-fort which dates from 500 BC.

Continue along the track and, shortly before it bends left, cross the stile on your right by the information board, Point **B**. Turn left alongside the fence to reach the Iron Age fort. At the trig point, cut across the centre of the fort and bear right along the path on top of the rampart and continue along the scarp edge. Admire the views west across Stourhead Estate to King Alfred's Tower on the skyline and southeast across the Blackmore Vale to the Dorset Downs beyond.

Keep the old granary workings to your right as you descend, picking up a path to a stile and into the car park. Keep left through the car park and follow the track to a gate. Proceed ahead, pass through Beech Clump, Point **C**, and continue on the wide track, crossing two stiles, to reach a gate and the B3092 opposite Drove Lodge. Turn left for a few paces, then look for the arrow on the opposite side of the road. Cross with care and take the footpath right through trees to a stile. Walk straight across parkland towards Stourhead House and join your outward route back to the main drive and Walk 43 at Point **7**.

# Westbury White Horse

| | |
|---|---|
| DISTANCE 4.25 miles (6.8km) | MINIMUM TIME 2hrs 30min |

ASCENT/GRADIENT 557ft (170m) ▲▲▲     LEVEL OF DIFFICULTY ✦✦✦

PATHS Field paths and downland tracks

LANDSCAPE Downland

SUGGESTED MAP OS Explorer 143 Warminster & Trowbridge

START/FINISH Grid reference: ST914523

DOG FRIENDLINESS On leads near grazing animals on Combe Bottom, Bratton Camp and Westbury Hill

PARKING Jubilee Hall in Tynings Lane, Bratton, just off B3098

PUBLIC TOILETS None on route

The most notable feature of Bratton, a large village in the shadow of a huge downland escarpment, is the Church of St James, arguably one of the most charming churches in the county. Reached by a series of steep steps, and nestling at the base of the chalk downland, it dates from about 1400 and is worth the climb to view the traces of Norman architecture and the wildly grinning gargoyles.

### ANGELS PLAYING MUSICAL INSTRUMENTS

The church looks magnificent, standing among the trees and set against this dramatic downland backdrop. The architecture is particularly striking; the arcades rest on clustered columns and the north transept has angels playing musical instruments or carrying shields. Looming above Bratton is Westbury Hill, which rises to a commanding height of 750ft (229m) above sea level and forms the dramatic western edge of Salisbury Plain. The views are tremendous, with the scarp slope dropping into the Vale of Pewsey, and on the horizon, on a clear day, you can see across Somerset to the Mendips and the Cotswolds. Dominating the hilltop is Bratton Castle, an Iron Age hill-fort covering 25 acres (10ha) of the plateau and defended by double banks and ditches rising to 35ft (11m). The long barrow inside the fort is a burial mound probably built before 3000 BC.

### SPIRIT OF A HORSE

Cut into the side of the hill, just below the castle ramparts, is Wiltshire's oldest and best known white horse, measuring 180ft (55m) long and 108ft (33m) high. This graceful hill figure is believed to have replaced a much earlier and cruder creature which local tradition states was cut in celebration of King Alfred's victory over the Danes at the Battle of Ethundun in AD 878. The present, well-proportioned animal was cut by a Mr Gee, steward to Lord Abingdon, in 1778, apparently because he objected to the primitive dog-like creature which had previously existed on Westbury Hill. The White Horse was remodelled in 1853 and restored 20 years later, with its most recent makeover in concrete, courtesy of Westbury Cement Works (the unmistakable industrial complex you can see in the valley below).

## STRIKING LANDMARKS

The south of England is renowned for its white horse chalk carvings. Up to 24 have been recorded in Britain with as many as 13 of them in Wiltshire at one time. Eight are still visible in the county, and a long distance trail links them all. The remaining carvings have been worn away by the passage of time or are hidden under turf, which has grown over them over the years. The Westbury White Horse is considered to be one of the best chalk carvings thanks to its striking position. The hilltop figures are usually created by the removal of the top layer of rather poor soil. This then reveals the white chalk beneath, which tends to contrast well with the short hill turf surrounding it. The result is particularly effective when the image is seen from some distance away.

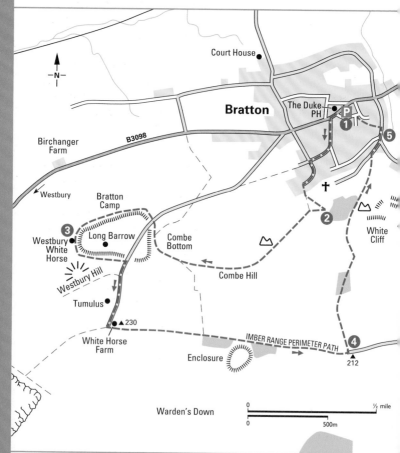

**1** Turn right out of the car park to the B3098. Turn left, then almost immediately left again up The Butts. Fork right into Upper Garston Lane by the Oratory of St Giles, then, just before the lane dips, take the path left, waymarked to the church. Descend steps, cross a brook, then climb steps to the church gates. Take the narrow path right and ascend through trees.

**2** When you reach a kissing gate on your left, turn right along a waymarked path; go through a kissing gate and bear left between lines of trees, climbing steeply up the scarp slope to the fence at the top. Keep right alongside the fence, continue through a gate, then turn right through a metal gate to follow a sunken track around the top of Combe Bottom. At the lane, turn left uphill and, as the lane bears left, fork right over a stile on to the outer rampart of Bratton Camp. Turn right to follow the outer rampart path to reach the Westbury White Horse hill figure.

**3** Shortly, leave the rampart and pass through a gate on to Westbury Hill. Keep to the path, passing to the left of benches, and soon reach a track. Turn left, pass the car park and turn right at the T-junction. Pass White Horse Farm, a collection of barns, and turn left along the track, following the Imber Range Perimeter Path. Keep to the track, passing a bridleway on the left, and continue to the next waymarked bridleway, by galvanized gates.

**4** Turn left here, follow the main track past a copse into a field and keep to the left-hand edge to a gate. Go through it and bear right, descending steeply on a sunken track towards Bratton. Go through a gate and drop down through trees, keeping ahead on reaching a metalled lane.

**5** Turn left at the T-junction, then bear left up a cobbled path (The Ball) between cottages. At the road, keep left back to the car park where the walk started.

WHERE TO EAT AND DRINK Refresh yourselves after this taxing downland walk at The Duke in Bratton, noted for its generous portions of home-cooked food, including excellent Sunday roasts, and for its range of ales.

WHAT TO SEE Make sure you pause at the viewpoint pillar on Westbury Hill, especially on a clear day, as you will be surprised just how far-reaching the view is. Walk this way in spring and early summer to see the grassy downland summit and slopes alive with chalk-loving plants such as bird's foot trefoil, and butterflies like the chalkhill blue.

WHILE YOU'RE THERE Make the short trip east along the B3098 to Edington to see the impressive, cathedral-like Priory Church of St Mary, St Katharine and All Saints. This architectural treasure was completed in 1361 as part of a priory founded by William of Edington, Bishop of Winchester, for Augustinian monks. There is much to marvel at, including a rare wooden screen of 1500 and a fine 17th-century plaster ceiling, so pick up a church guide.

# Corsham and its Park

DISTANCE 4 miles (6.4km)   MINIMUM TIME 2hrs

ASCENT/GRADIENT 114ft (35m) ▲▲▲   LEVEL OF DIFFICULTY ✚✚✚

PATHS Field paths and country lanes, many stiles

LANDSCAPE Town streets, gently undulating parkland, farmland

SUGGESTED MAP AA Leisure Map 15 Swindon & Devizes

START/FINISH Grid reference: ST871704

DOG FRIENDLINESS Can be off lead in Corsham Park, except where grazing

PARKING Long-stay car park in Newlands Lane

PUBLIC TOILETS Short-stay car park by shopping precinct

Warm, cream-coloured Bath stone characterises this little market town on the southern edge of the Cotswolds. An air of prosperity pervades the streets where the 15th-century Flemish gabled cottages and baroque-pedimented 17th-century Hungerford Almshouses mix with larger Georgian residences. Architectural historian Nikolaus Pevsner wrote: 'Corsham has no match in Wiltshire for the wealth of good houses.' The town owes its inheritance to the once-thriving industries of cloth manufacture and stone quarrying in the 17th and 18th centuries.

## ARCHITECTURAL DELIGHTS

Explore the heart of the town before setting off across Corsham Park, as many of the fine stone buildings along the High Street, Church Street and Priory Street have been well preserved. Begin your town stroll at the Heritage Centre in the High Street (No. 31), where displays and exhibits present the stories of the weaving industry and quarrying of the golden Bath stone, which was used to create the architectural legacy of the town. In fact, No. 31 once belonged to a prosperous 18th-century clothier, and No. 70 (now an electrical shop) was the workhouse providing labour for the cloth industry. The Town Hall was formerly the market hall with one storey and open arches before being converted in 1882. North of the post office you will see the unspoilt line of 17th-century weavers' cottages. Known as the Flemish Buildings, this was the centre of the cloth industry where the Flemish weavers settled following religious persecution in their homeland. In Church Street, note the gabled cottages of the 18th-century weavers, with their ornate porches and a door on the first floor for taking in the raw wool.

## CORSHAM COURT – THE METHUEN FAMILY HOME

The finest of the houses is Corsham Court, a splendid Elizabethan mansion built in 1582. It was bought in 1745 by Paul Methuen, a wealthy clothier and ancestor of the present owner, to house the family's collection of 16th- and 17th-century Italian and Flemish Master paintings and statuary. The house and park are principally the work of 'Capability' Brown, John Nash and Thomas Bellamy. Brown built the gabled wings that house the state rooms and magnificent 72ft (22m) long picture gallery and laid out the park, including the avenues, Gothic bathhouse and the 13-acre (5ha) lake.

Finish the walk with a tour of the house. You will see the outstanding collection of over 140 paintings, including pictures by Rubens, Turner, Reynolds and Van Dyck, fine statuary and bronzes, and the famous collection of English furniture, notably pieces by Robert Adam and Thomas Chippendale. You may recognise the house as the backdrop for the 1993 film *The Remains of the Day*, starring Anthony Hopkins.

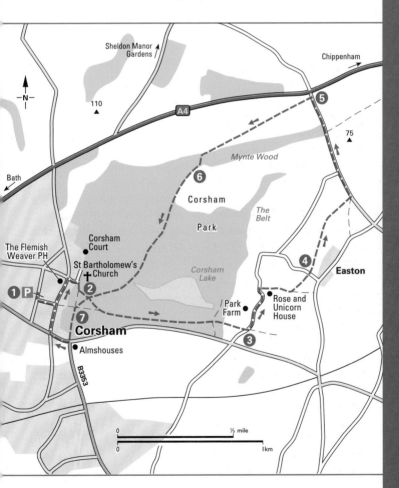

❶ Turn left out of the car park, then left again along Post Office Lane to reach the High Street. Turn left, pass the tourist information centre and turn right into Church Street. Pass the impressive entrance to Corsham Court on your left, and as you approach St Bartholomew's churchyard turn right to a kissing gate and avenue.

**2** Follow the path left after a few paces and walk ahead across Corsham Park, passing Corsham Lake, to reach a stile and gate. Go slightly right along a fenced path beside a track to a kissing gate and proceed across a field to a stile and lane.

**3** Turn left, pass Park Farm, a splendid stone farmhouse on your left, and shortly take the waymarked footpath right along a drive to pass Rose and Unicorn House. Cross a stile and follow the right-hand field-edge to a stile, then bear half left to a stone stile in the field corner. Head straight across the field to a further stile and lane.

**4** Take the footpath opposite, bearing half left to a stone stile to the left of a cottage. Maintain direction, passing to the right of a spring, and go through a field entrance to follow the path along the left-hand side of a field to a stile in the corner. Turn left

along the road for 0.5 miles (800m) to reach the A4.

**5** Go through the gate in the wall on your left and follow the worn path right, across the centre of parkland pasture to a metal kissing gate. Proceed ahead to reach a kissing gate on the edge of woodland. Follow the wide path, bearing half right to a stile.

**6** Keep ahead on a worn path across the parkland and along the field-edge to a gate. Continue to a further gate with fine views right to Corsham Court. To enter St Bartholomew's churchyard, make for a gate in the right-hand wall. Otherwise continue ahead to a stile and gate.

**7** Turn left down the avenue of trees to a gate and the town centre, noting the stone almshouses on your left. Turn right along Lacock Road and then right again along the pedestrianised High Street. Turn left back along Post Office Lane to the car park.

**WHERE TO EAT AND DRINK** Corsham is well served by pubs, restaurants and cafes, notably The Flemish Weaver pub on the High Street, serving modern food and excellent Bath Ales.

**WHAT TO SEE** Note the Folly along Church Street, an artificial ruin set with church windows, built by Nash in 1800 to hide Ethelred House from Corsham Court. Seek out the grave of Sarah Jarvis behind St Bartholomew's Church; she died in 1703 aged 107 having grown a new set of teeth! A plaque at 38 High Street informs that Sir Michael Tippett, one of Britain's greatest composers, lived there in the 1960s.

**WHILE YOU'RE THERE** Visit Sheldon Manor Gardens (3 miles/4.8km north), Wiltshire's oldest inhabited manor house and sole survivor of a deserted medieval village. Dating from 1282, this well-preserved Plantagenet house has been a family home for 700 years and features a 13th-century porch, a 15th-century chapel and beautiful informal terraced gardens.

# On Salisbury Plain

DISTANCE 6 miles (9.7km)    MINIMUM TIME 2hrs 30min

ASCENT/GRADIENT 180ft (55m) ▲▲▲    LEVEL OF DIFFICULTY ✦✦✦

PATHS Byway, bridleway, footpath, several stretches of road

LANDSCAPE Downland and farmland. North of the B390 the land is owned by the MOD with strict bylaws. South of the road the land is civilian-owned

SUGGESTED MAP OS Explorer 143 Warminster & Trowbridge

START/FINISH Grid reference: ST993441

DOG FRIENDLINESS On lead and under close control on outward leg of walk and on road sections

PARKING In vicinity of Chitterne Church

PUBLIC TOILETS None on route

When you think of Salisbury Plain the image that usually springs to mind is an undulating chalk plateau, a hostile, desolate place with much evidence of military activity and a tangible air of ancient mystery. Salisbury Plain and the whole of North Wessex were once the most heavily populated areas in the country, inhabited by the people of the late Stone Age. Today the Plain is one of the loneliest and least populated tracts of land in the south of England, if not all of Britain. It has a timeless quality and there is a very good reason for this. The Ministry of Defence first conducted exercises on Salisbury Plain in the late 1890s and between then and World War II sizeable chunks of land were acquired for training. The MOD now own 150 square miles (390sq km) of land here, making it the largest military training area in the UK. Of this about 39 square miles (100sq km) is permanently off limits to the public, with access greatly restricted in other areas.

## DESERTED VILLAGE

As military use of Salisbury Plain increased, new camps sprang into existence. Imber, one of the region's best-known villages, was evacuated to enable training for Operation Overlord, crucial to the outcome of World War II, to take place in 1944. The villagers never returned to their homes after the war and the remains of Imber continue to be used for training. One of the best ways to explore Salisbury Plain is by following the 30-mile (48km) Imber Range Perimeter Path, which, although it keeps to the edge of the Plain, does evoke a strong sense of adventure and give a real flavour of the area. The views from the trail are particularly impressive. The outward leg of this walk follows the Imber Range Perimeter Path over the southern slopes of the Plain.

## HAVEN FOR WILDLIFE

The backdrop is dramatic and in places you can see how Salisbury Plain has remained untouched by modern intensive farming. As a result it is one of the last surviving chalk grassland areas in Britain, probably Europe. The entire region is designated a Site of Special Scientific Interest (SSSI). Salisbury Plain also includes various archaeological sites, which have thankfully remained intact over the years, and through lack of use in recent years the place has become a fascinating haven for wildlife. Twenty pairs of stone curlews breed on the Plain and other breeding species include buzzards, barn owls, nightingales and corn buntings.

## LITERARY AND ARTISTIC ASSOCIATIONS

Salisbury Plain has captured the imagination of some of our greatest writers and artists, too. William Wordsworth and Thomas Hardy wrote about this unique landscape and Constable painted it.

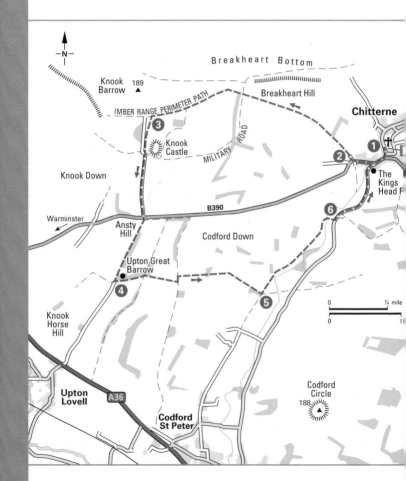

❶ From the parking area turn left to the T-junction. Keep right, signposted Warminster and Codford, pass The Kings Head and continue along the main road through the village. When the road bends left veer right to join a byway (Imber Range Perimeter Path).

❷ Follow the sunken track between trees and further up they give way to open downland. Cross a track and keep ahead to a copse. On reaching the Military Road continue on the Imber Range Perimeter Path. After about 200yds (183m), bear left at the fence corner and continue on the byway. Avoid a turning down to a small copse enclosing farm outbuildings and head up the slope to the next junction.

❸ Turn left, heading south on a byway, and re-cross the Military Road at a staggered junction. Continue south on the byway, passing barns on the left. Cross the B390 road and follow the byway as it climbs steadily alongside woodland on the left. Pass a corrugated barn on the right and after about 120yds (110m) swing left through a metal gate by a cattle grid.

❹ Follow the byway with trees and the outline of Upton Great Barrow on the left. On reaching a cattle grid and track junction keep ahead on the byway to the next gate and cattle grid. Turn left, then right after about 75yds (69m) to follow a bridleway. Across the field go through several gates and maintain direction, heading towards trees and keeping fencing on your left. Follow the path as it bends right in the field corner and drop down to a metal gate. Pass through it and follow the field-edge downhill to a concrete track.

❺ Turn left, where the bridleway runs straight on, and follow the track to where it curves left by a gate. Keep over to the right and follow the field boundary. Make for a gate on the far side of the field and enter the next pasture. Follow the right-hand edge all the way to a stile on the right.

❻ Cross it and keep right to a footbridge in the field corner. The bridge has stiles either end of it. Cross them and continue along the field edge for a short distance to the next stile. Cross it to the road and turn left, back to Chitterne. At the junction near The Kings Head, turn right and return to the church and parking area.

WHERE TO EAT AND DRINK The Kings Head at Chitterne, at the start and finish of the walk, offers a variety of snacks and meals, including a Sunday roast and fish and chips. There is also a range of ales.

WHAT TO SEE If time permits continue on the Imber Range Perimeter Path at the end of Point ❷ to reach a superb viewpoint with stunning vistas over distant rounded hills, including Cotley Hill, Battlesbury Hill and Scratchbury Hill. There are also good views to the north across the heart of Salisbury Plain. The 360-degree views from here are so extensive that when visibility is good you can see up to at least 15 miles (24km).

WHILE YOU'RE THERE As you follow the byway south of the B390 look to the west, where there are spectacular views towards the village of Heytesbury. This was the home of the World War I poet Siegfried Sassoon who lived there until his death in 1967, having earlier been stationed locally.

# Kennet & Avon Canal at Bradford-on-Avon

| | | | |
|---|---|---|---|
| **DISTANCE** 3.25 miles (5.3km) | | **MINIMUM TIME** 1hr 45min | |

**ASCENT/GRADIENT** 164ft (50m) ▲▲▲    **LEVEL OF DIFFICULTY** ✦✦✦

**PATHS** Tow path, field and woodland paths, metalled lanes

**LANDSCAPE** Canal, river valley, wooded hillsides, town streets

**SUGGESTED MAP** AA Walker's Map 25 Bristol, Bath & The Mendips

**START/FINISH** Grid reference: ST824606

**DOG FRIENDLINESS** On lead through town

**PARKING** Bradford-on-Avon station car park (charge)

**PUBLIC TOILETS** Station car park and St Margaret's car park

Set in the wooded Avon Valley, Bradford is one of Wiltshire's loveliest towns, combining historical charm, appealing architecture and dramatic topography. It is often likened to a miniature Bath, with the same honey-coloured limestone, elegant terraces and steep winding streets that rise sharply away from the river. Historically a 'broad ford' across the Avon, the original Iron Age settlement was expanded by the Romans and Saxons, the latter giving Bradford its greatest treasure, St Laurence's Church. The Avon was spanned by a fine stone bridge in the 13th century – two of its arches survive in the present 17th-century structure – and by the 1630s Bradford had grown into a powerful centre for the cloth and woollen industries.

## WEALTHY WOOL TOWN

Exploring the riverside and the lanes, alleys and flights of steps up the north slope of the town is most rewarding. Beautiful terraces are lined with elegant 18th-century merchants' houses with walled gardens, and charming 17th- and 18th-century weavers' cottages. The wealth that made all this building possible came from the manufacture of woollen cloth. Bradford's medieval prosperity is reflected in the size of the magnificent 14th-century tithe barn at Barton Farm.

With the development of mechanisation, the wool trade moved from individual houses to large water- and steam-driven mills along the banks of the Avon. At the time that the Kennet and Avon Canal was built, in 1810, the town supported around 30 mills; some of these buildings survive, in various degrees of restoration or disrepair, today. With the centre of the wool trade shifting north to Yorkshire, the industry declined during the 19th century and the last of the mills closed in 1905. The town is now prosperous once again with tourists and new residents, many commuting to Bath, Bristol and even London.

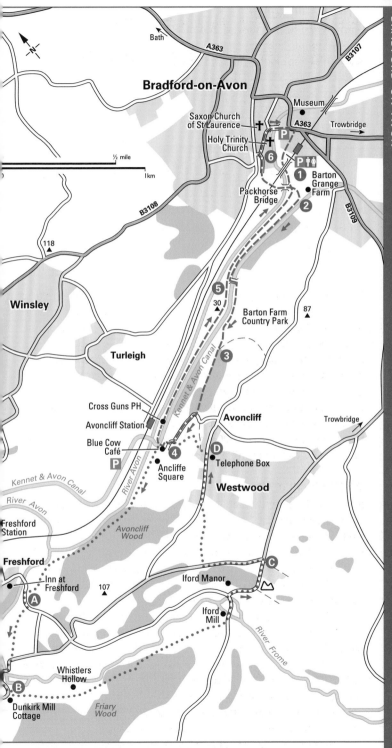

Bath

A363

B3107

**Bradford-on-Avon**

Museum

Saxon Church of St Laurence

A363

Trowbridge

Holy Trinity Church

**6**

P

P ♀♂

½ mile

1 km

**1** Barton Grange Farm

Packhorse Bridge

**2**

B3109

118

**5**

B3108

30

Barton Farm Country Park

87

**Winsley**

**Turleigh**

Kennet & Avon Canal

**3**

Cross Guns PH

Avoncliff Station

**Avoncliff**

Trowbridge

Blue Cow Café

P

**4**

**D**

Telephone Box

Ancliffe Square

**Westwood**

River Avon

Kennet & Avon Canal

River Avon

Freshford Station

Avoncliff Wood

**Freshford**

Inn at Freshford

107

Iford Manor

**C**

**A**

Iford Mill

River Frome

Whistlers Hollow

**B**

Dunkirk Mill Cottage

Friary Wood

## JEWEL IN THE CROWN

Down by the river is the tiny Saxon Church of St Laurence. Founded by St Aldhelm, Abbot of Malmesbury, in AD 700, the present structure dates from the 10th century. For centuries it was forgotten. The chancel became a house, the nave a school, and the west wall part of a factory building. The true origins and purpose of the site were only rediscovered in 1858.

❶ Walk to the end of the car park, away from the station, and follow the path left beneath the railway and beside the River Avon. Enter Barton Farm Country Park and keep to the path across a grassy area to a junction of paths. With the packhorse bridge right, keep ahead, passing to the right of Barton Grange Farm and up to the Kennet & Avon Canal.

❷ Turn right along the tow path, signed to Avoncliff. Cross the bridge over the canal in 0.5 miles (800m) and follow the path right to a footbridge and kissing gate. Proceed along the right-hand field-edge to a further kissing gate, then bear diagonally left uphill, away from the canal, to a third kissing gate.

❸ Follow the path through the edge of woodland. Keep to the path as it bears left uphill through the trees to reach a metalled lane. Turn right and walk steeply downhill to Avoncliff and the canal.

❹ Don't cross the aqueduct; instead, go past the Blue Cow Café, descend the steps on your right and pass beneath the canal. Keep right by The Cross Guns and join the tow path towards Bradford-on-Avon. Continue for 0.75 miles (1.2km) to the bridge crossed on your outward route.

❺ Bear off left downhill along a metalled track and follow it beside the River Avon back into Barton Farm Country Park. Cross the packhorse bridge and the railway and follow the walled path uphill and right into Barton Orchard. Bear right at the end down the alleyway to Church Street.

❻ Follow Church Street down past the Holy Trinity Church and the Saxon Church of St Laurence. Cross the footbridge and walk through St Margaret's car park to the road. Turn right, then right again into the station car park.

WHERE TO EAT AND DRINK  In Bradford-on-Avon, try The Cottage Co-Operative Cafe in Weaver's Walk, The Swan Hotel in Church Street, and The Canal Tavern or The Lock Inn Café Bar on Frome Road. The Cross Guns at Avoncliff offers pub food and a terraced riverside garden. The Blue Cow Café serves soup, baguettes and cakes (open weekends only in winter).

WHAT TO SEE  Note the small, dome-shaped building at the south end of Town Bridge. Called the 'Chapel', it was, in fact, a lock-up or 'blind house' containing two cells with iron bedsteads for prisoners.

WHILE YOU'RE THERE  Linger at Barton Farm Country Park to view the craft shops in the medieval farm buildings, and marvel at the great beams and rafters of Bradford's magnificent tithe barn.

*Right: Inside the Tithe Barn in Bradford-on-Avon (Walk 48)*

# Through the Frome Valley

DISTANCE 3.5 miles (5.7km)   MINIMUM TIME 2hrs

ASCENT/GRADIENT 170ft (52m) ▲▲▲   LEVEL OF DIFFICULTY ✦✦✦

SEE MAP AND INFORMATION PANEL FOR WALK 48

At Avoncliff (Point ❹ on Walk 48), drop down with the Blue Cow Café on your left, disregard the tow path signs and keep ahead along the track to pass Ancliffe Square. As it veers left, maintain your direction through the gate and trees. Go through a gate and soon walk beside the River Avon to reach another gate. Pass through woodland to a gate, then head across water-meadows to a gate and lane and the River Frome at Freshford, Point ❹.

Turn left, climb a stile on your right and bear half left across the field towards buildings, to a stile and lane. Turn right, walk beside the river and cross the bridge. Continue uphill and take the bridle path left in front of Dunkirk Mill Cottage, Point ❹. Bear right, then take the bridle path left opposite Middle House.

Continue to a gate, keep left down to a track and then turn left. Turn right opposite River House. Keep left through a field to a gate and walk through Friary Wood to a stile. Turn right along the field edge for 0.5 miles (800m) to a stile and lane. Turn left, pass Iford Mill and cross the river bridge to Iford Manor Gardens. Bear right and walk steeply uphill to a junction, Point ❹.

Turn left along the verge for 0.25 miles (400m) and take the sometimes muddy bridle path right, signed 'Upper Westwood'. At a lane, turn right through Upper Westwood. Turn left opposite the telephone box, Point ❹, then, where the lane curves left, take the left of two footpaths ahead. Avoid left turnings. Walk downhill through the edge of woodland. Go through a gate, cross a drive and follow the lane left, downhill back to Avoncliff to rejoin Walk 48.

# Bradford-on-Avon to Bath

| | |
|---|---|
| DISTANCE 9.25 miles (14.9km) | MINIMUM TIME 3hrs 45min |

ASCENT/GRADIENT Negligible ▲▲▲     LEVEL OF DIFFICULTY ✦✦✦

PATHS Canal tow path

LANDSCAPE River valley and urban area

SUGGESTED MAP Map OS Explorers 155 Bristol and Bath;
156 Chippenham & Bradford-on-Avon

START/FINISH Grid reference: ST824606 (on Explorer 156)

DOG FRIENDLINESS No real problems; keep under control through
Bath streets/roads

PARKING Bradford-on-Avon Station pay-and-display car park

PUBLIC TOILETS Bradford-on-Avon Station car park and Bath Spa station

Bradford-on-Avon lies on the Kennet and Avon Canal, which stretches 87 miles (140km) from the River Avon at Bristol to the River Thames at Reading. Now fully restored, the canal offers some of the best-loved walking in Wiltshire. Between Bradford and Bath it passes through steep wooded hillsides that rise 400ft (122m) above the Avon Valley, arguably the finest natural landscape along the length of the canal. But there is far more than just great scenery for you to savour on this memorable lengthy ramble to Bath. You will discover some exceptional canal structures, notable restored wharves, magnificent aqueducts, a 19th-century pumping station and ornately decorated tunnels.

## ENGINEERING WORKS

At Bradford-on-Avon the canal company built two wharves, one below and one above the lock. A lock was required to raise the level of the canal to that of the Wilts and Berks Canal at Semington. On the upper wharf, a stone and timber structure was built and alongside it remains the original dry dock, now in use again.

With great skill, the engineer John Rennie took the canal along the winding River Avon Valley crossing the River Avon twice via substantial aqueducts. Avoncliff Aqueduct was built between 1797 and 1801 to take the canal across the valley to the north side. It is 110yds (100m) long and features three arches, a solid parapet and balustrade ends. The Bath stone has not weathered well and has suffered from casual repair work and patching in brick.

Perhaps the most impressive of the masonry structures on the canal, Dundas Aqueduct stands as a fitting memorial to the architectural and engineering skill of John Rennie. Built in 1804, this fine classical stone aqueduct carries the canal 64ft (19.5m) above the River Avon on a graceful wide arch spanning 65ft (19.8m) and framed by paired giant pilasters. Brassknocker Basin marks the junction of the Kennet and Avon Canal with the Somerset Coal Canal, opened in 1801 to run 10 miles (16.1km) to the mines at Paulton and Radstock. It was taken over by a railway company and closed in 1898. The first 0.25 miles (400m) was restored between 1986 and 1988 for moorings.

## ENVIRONMENTALLY FRIENDLY

The waterwheel at Claverton Pumping Station began working in 1813 and harnessed the power of the River Avon to raise water from the Avon to the canal some 48ft (14.63m) higher on the landscape. It is the only one of its kind on British canals and is a fine example of late Georgian–Regency architecture and engineering. Now fully restored, it is open to the public from April to October at weekends and on Wednesdays (pumping roughly two Sundays each month).

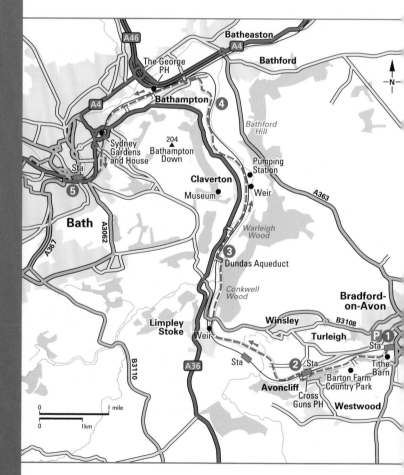

**1** Walk to the end of the car park away from the station and follow the path left beneath the railway and beside the river. Enter Barton Farm Country Park and keep to the path across a grassy area to an information board. Veer left, ascending, and pass to the right of the tithe barn, using steps to reach the Kennet and Avon Canal. Turn right along the tow path for 1.75 miles (2.8km) to Avoncliff.

**2** Follow the zig-zag in front of the Cross Guns pub to pass beneath the canal. Ascend the steps immediately to your left and then another set of stone steps on the left to rejoin the canal tow path. Go left and proceed for 3 miles (4.8km) to the Dundas Aqueduct.

**3** After stopping to admire the aqueduct, cross the bridge over the canal and continue for 1.25 miles (2km) to Claverton Pumping Station. Continue on the canal tow path through the now very rural Avon Valley, with all eras of transport modes in sight – river, canal, railway and road – to reach Bathampton and the swing bridge (No. 182).

**4** Keep to the tow path as it eventually leads you through the attractive suburbs of Bath, probably the least stressful and least busy route into the heart of the city. The canal passes through Sydney Gardens (there is a small gate to access the gardens along this part of the tow path), go through a tunnel which takes you underneath Sydney House, then up some stone steps and cross the canal at the back of Sydney House to continue the walk on the opposite side of the canal. At the bottom of Bathwick Hill, cross the road and canal and go through an iron gate to go down some steps and access the tow path again. After passing five locks you will reach the A36.

**5** Cross the road and continue on the tow path. At lock 8/9, cross the road and continue along the tow path to lock No. 7 (the canal is now on the right). At lock No. 7 the canal meets the River Avon. Do not follow the riverside path ahead, instead move left to reach the pavement beside the road and turn right to cross the iron footbridge over the Avon to Bath Spa Station. Return to Bradford-on-Avon via the half-hourly train service (hourly on Sundays).

**WHERE TO EAT AND DRINK** Try the Hop Pole Inn at Limpley Stoke or, further along the walk, there is a cafe and museum at Brassknocker Basin. For a quick pit stop The George at Bathampton is right on the canal or, if you can keep going for those last few miles, there is a plethora of excellent cafes and restaurants in Bath.

**WHAT TO SEE** Note the tow rope marks etched into the tight corner of Avoncliff Aqueduct and the two old flock mills on the River Avon. Look for the 0.25-mile (400m) posts showing the distance from the River Thames at Reading, and the cast iron crane at Dundas Wharf.

**WHILE YOU'RE THERE** Spend some time exploring Georgian Bath. Highlights include the 15th-century abbey, the Roman Baths, the Pump Room, Pulteney Bridge, the Circus and the Royal Crescent.

*Overleaf: Town bridge over the river at Bradford-on-Avon (Walk 50)*